D0810726

FAILURE: THE WOMB OF SUCCESS

Samuel R. Chand
David C. Cooper
Collette L. Gunby
Wiley Jackson, Jr.
Eddie L. Long
Woodrow Walker, II
and others

Edited by: Cecil Murphey
Gloria Spencer

Mall Publishing Co.

THE PRINTED WORD THE PLANTED SEED

Niles, Illinois

Failure: The Womb of Success is a publication of Beulah Heights Bible College. For further information or to schedule a follow up please contact:

Dr. Samuel R. Chand, President
Beulah Heights Bible College
P.O. Box 18145
Atlanta, GA 30316
1-888-777-BHBC (toll free)
1-404-627-0702 (fax)
samuel.chand@beulah.org (email)

Produced by Mall Publishing Co.
Niles, Illinois 60714

ISBN 1-57921-168-2
Library of Congress Catalog Card Number: 98-88759

FAILURE: THE WOMB OF SUCCESS

The Story Behind the Book

It was the first Monday in August 1985. Mondays can either be real good or real bad for pastors depending on the day before Monday—Sunday! Sunday is the day the self-worth and even the calling of the pastor are tested to its limits. An experienced pastor has counseled wisely, "Never resign on a Monday!"

On this particular Monday, I walked up to a few pastor friends who were gathered in the parking lot of the Conference center. The annual denominational conference was about to begin. The typical Monday morning pastor's conversation was in full bloom.

"So, how many did you have in church yesterday?" was the operating question.

Now, we all know that the question is usually asked by pastors who had a "good" Sunday, and this is the way they can let others know how well they did. Actually, it is a very self-serving question. It is not about the questioned; it is about the questioner!

The respondent, who usually had a "bad" Sunday responds by shuffling his feet, clearing his throat, and saying something like, "We've had a lot of sickness in our area and seems like so many people were out on vacation ..."

This one-upmanship in the parking lot that Monday morning got the best of me. So, as a junior member of the clergy, I timidly asked, "Do any of you have low Sundays? Do you ever get discouraged? Do you ever feel like giving up? Do you ever wonder if it's worth it?" As soon as the words left my mouth, I knew I had said the wrong thing! Why deal with reality when denial serves us so well?

The book in your hands was born on that Monday morning in that parking lot. The accounts in the book finally answer the question that were asked in the parking lot and remind us that failure is the womb of success. As you read this book, you will laugh and you will weep. You will shake your head in agreement as well as amazement.

Failure is not a popular subject. Go to your nearest bookstore and look for the shelf marked FAILURE; that shelf does not exist! Everyone wants to talk about success (it sells), but we all know we fail at more things than we succeed at. So let's talk about it!

This book will get you started.

Samuel R. Chand
Coordinator and collaborator of this book

Cecil Murphey
Freelance Writer with over seventy published books,
Tucker, Georgia

The Dark Side of Ministry

BY CECIL MURPHEY

Cecil Murphey, a full-time writer, fiction and nonfiction, since 1984.

Learn to fail.

I wish someone had said those words to me when I trained for ministry. During those days of study and preparation, I heard stories of victories. Teachers pointed out miracles in the Old Testament and healings in the Gospels. We read about mass conversions in Acts. I heard testimonies of Paul, John, and modern saints overcoming the worst possible obstacles.

And those are part of ministry—they're the bright side.

Somebody forgot to tell me about the dark side of ministry.

I've had my share of those dark times and so has everyone who has written a chapter in this book. The dark times are when we wondered what we had done wrong. "If I'm serving Jesus Christ," we asked ourselves, "could I have messed up so badly?" Or we wondered what could God do with ones like us who failed so frequently.

We moaned for being weak. We confessed and reminded ourselves that we'd never change unless God did something for us.

Yes, we all know the dark side of ministry.

As a missionary in Kenya for six years and a pastor for fourteen years, I failed with regularity.

I didn't like failure then, and I don't like it now. But I've learned that failures are part of the growing process. Nobody reaches spiritual maturity without failure—a lot of failure—along the way.

Today I can talk about my shortcomings and so do the people who wrote chapters in this book. We can talk about them because they were part of our spiritual education and maturing in Christ. Because we know our past failures, we are assured that we'll have present and future ones. Those experiences also assure us of God's forgiveness and grace.

This book is about the dark side of ministry. In the pages that follow, you'll read personal testimonies of some of God's most faithful and dedicated servants. You'll read about their dark sides, their failures, and their mistakes.

As you read of their failures, bear in mind that they are successful and victorious today because they stumbled, got back up, and continued onward. For them, failure became a vital ingredient for success.

As I prepared this introduction, I thought about my failures—which wasn't easy. Those I thought of involved the wrong use of words—speaking unwisely. *Unwisely* is my cover-up word for saying that sometimes I was insensitive, thoughtless, unkind, or meanspirited.

Here's a quick take on some of my failures.

* I had gotten to know an African well, and we had a lot of fun teasing each other. One day I said, "You were a naughty boy." I wasn't sensitive enough to realize that the word *boy* offended him.

* Dennis, an elder in our church, had hurt my feelings. Instead of going to him, I told someone else. It was unkind of me, and I believe it prejudiced that man against Dennis.

* The fiancé of Alice, my wife's best friend, wrote me a letter asking what I thought of Alice. I told him. What I said represented my true feelings, but the words were harsh and judgmental. Looking back, I realize that just because he asked, didn't mean I had to tell him. To make it worse, he showed my letter to Alice, and she then turned against my wife as well.

As I listed my times of missing the mark, I paused and asked, "God, show me more failures."

I waited in silence. Inside my head I heard a voice whisper, "Failures? I don't remember any."

That's the best thing about failures, isn't it?

God forgets them.

Dr. Samuel R. Chand
President, Beulah Heights Bible College,
Atlanta, Georgia

CHAPTER 1

Five Chapters of Failure

BY DR. SAMUEL R. CHAND

I could write my own book of personal failures because I've experienced them. If I were going to write such a book, here are five failures I would have to include.

The first chapter would have to go back to my childhood. As a boy growing up in India, I knew very early that I wasn't athletically coordinated. As it happens in most gym classes, the best players pick out their teams. I hated when that happened because I knew that inevitably I would be the last one picked. My team captain usually made fun of me because he was stuck with me.

Although I got older, I never got any more athletically coordinated. By the time I reached high school, athletics seemed the only way to show others, especially girls, how we boys were going to be men in the world. By then, I had withdrawn from sports and avoided them as much as possible. But deep inside, I wanted to be athletic and play like the other guys.

My chance finally came—at age 29. By then, I had become the pastor of the Full Gospel Assembly in Hartford, Michigan. We had our own softball team, and as their pastor I decided to join them as a member. I had played softball but I'd never been good at it. I didn't talk much about playing, but I knew it was going to be a wonderful time for me. At last, I could play softball like other men. I bought my own numbered T-shirt with Full Gospel Assembly printed on the back. I bought a good pair of shoes. To make me a real ball player, I bought the first softball mitt I had ever owned. I even bought oil for the glove and spent a lot of time massaging the oil into the leather.

Because I would start with the disadvantage of not having played softball well, several times before our first practice, my wife, Brenda, went into the parking lot with me. She pitched me the ball. It wasn't easy, but I finally learned to catch it—well, most of the time. I can remember in school when the only position I played would be in a place where the coach believed the ball would not come, and that often meant being moved in the middle of the game to a safer position.

Now I was ready to play ball! At last, I would show that I was like all the other men around me. But my fantasies didn't come true.

I played outfield. Despite all the practice with Brenda in the parking lot, when that ball zoomed into the field, I never could catch it. After the second or third game, a player would hit a fly ball, and I'd hear my player-friends yell as the ball came their way, "I got it! I got it!"

Under my breath, I'd say, "Yeah, you got it! You got it!"

Despite trying to do my best and praying a lot, my playing never improved. When our team was at bat, I never hit a home run, although one time I did get a one-base hit. In the outfield, I'd hear myself praying, "Lord, if you love me you won't let a ball come my way."

One day, Richard Matheny, the coach of the team, called me aside after a game. He put his arm around my shoulder and said, "Pastor, you've been preaching a lot about letting God use your gifts. Maybe one of the gifts you don't have is playing softball."

I couldn't even look him in the eyes when he talked. It wasn't as bad as being laughed at by my schoolmates, but it hurt anyway.

I had failed again.

"Look, you have a good strong voice," he said. "Here's what you can do. You can stand on the sideline, yell for us, and encourage us."

"All right," I said and tried to smile. I felt as if I had experienced the worst failure of my life. I had been dismissed from the softball team at my own church. I felt humiliated, even though I was happy not to be out there on the field and fumbling whenever a ball came my way.

"Well, here it happens again," I said to myself as I walked alone across the field. "Nothing has changed."

It was the same old pattern again—I just couldn't make it.

I began to wonder how to put a nice, positive spin on this so I didn't look bad. How would I cover for this failure? How would I smile through the whole thing? I wasn't angry at anybody, only disappointed in myself for not being able to measure up.

For the rest of that season, I went to most of the games—always arriving after they had started. When I showed up, I wore a suit and dress shoes. I never carried my mitt with me so that if they were short of players they wouldn't be able to call on me.

It's only softball, I told myself again and again—and it was. At the time, however, and for the rest of that summer, whenever I thought of softball, I thought of my failure to measure up.

The second chapter of failure began in 1979. Brenda and I met when we were students at Beulah Heights Bible College and married April 14, 1979. A couple of weeks after our wedding, we moved from Atlanta to Gresham, Oregon to become the associate youth pastor of Shiloh Assembly.

Shiloh Assembly, which was a small congregation, offered me the best they could: an apartment and paid utilities. Brenda and I had no money, and we were driving a 1969 LeMans that needed constant repairs.

When we agreed to move to Gresham, I knew I would have to find a job right away. That didn't bother me; I was positive I could land something quickly. I didn't. I looked for a job month after month and didn't find any kind of job I was qualified for. I went through private agencies, public agencies, government agencies, and direct contacts. I spent every weekday following up newspaper ads and leads from friends. The people at the agencies got to know me well. As much as they could, they made referrals, but nothing came of my efforts.

I tried to enter the job market with a BA in Biblical Education. Aware that that wasn't very marketable, when I talked to any agency or prospective employer, I stressed that I dealt well with people, even though I had no technical skills.

In contrast, Brenda, who had office skills, looked at job opportunities for three days; by then she had choices about which job to take.

Although happy that Brenda had a job and her income helped to pay our bills, the longer it took me to find a job, the more worthless I felt. Many wives worked, and it wasn't the issue of money. But in India where I grew up, I had been taught that a man didn't send his wife out to work. He was the provider, and I wasn't supporting my family, so I was failing.

I vividly remember one morning about a month into the whole odyssey of not being able to find a job. Brenda kissed me goodbye and left for work. I was still in pajamas. It was too early to go out, but just the contrast of our clothes filled me with depression.

To make it worse, the church didn't always receive enough money to pay our rent. When that happened, the senior pastor would say from the pulpit on Sunday morning something like, "Sam's rent is due now." The church would take an extra offering. I felt humiliated every time.

Finally I told him, "The church called you and it pays your salary, and you don't have to announce your bills. You pay for electricity and phone without special offerings. My rent should be like that—just another bill of the church."

My protest didn't make much of an impact. As long as we lived in Gresham, the practice continued.

Chapter three took place the following year. We moved from Oregon to Hartford, Michigan, to pastor the Full Gospel Assembly. That was the church where Brenda had been saved in 1970. Her parents lived in that same town.

When we arrived in Hartford at the end of August 1980, about thirty people attended worship on Sundays. Growth began almost immediately. Within the next four Sundays, the attendance had doubled. By the end of 1980, we averaged about one hundred in worship. Things were going well; people told me what a great pastor I was, and I began to believe it.

For the church to grow, especially since it had been there a long time, it meant the pastor had to spend a lot of time visiting in homes and meeting with people. My days were so filled that I left home early in the morning and sometimes Brenda would already be in bed when I came home.

Besides that, she was pregnant and due around October 10. She wasn't happy with my being gone all those long hours while she was home alone. Several times she said, "I need some time, too."

"I'll do better," I promised and meant it. For three or four nights I came home earlier, but I was soon into my old patterns again.

Sometimes when I came home, Brenda was crying. Only weeks earlier, however, I had read in *Reader's Digest* that women go through hormonal changes when they're pregnant, so I assumed that was the problem.

To show how unaware I was, once Brenda asked, long before the days of pagers and cellular phones, "What if I go into labor and you're not here?" The closest hospital was in St. Joe, Michigan, a good half-hour drive away.

"Just call your folks," I answered. (They lived three miles away.) "They'll take you and leave me a note." Even as I share this, I think about what a jerk I was and how messed up my priorities were, and I didn't even realize it. I think I was so caught up in the growth of our congregation that all my buttons had been pushed and my ego was inflated.

It came to a head the first Saturday night in October. I came home around 10:00 p.m. To my surprise, Brenda was not crying. She sat in the living room, smiled at me, and seemed very much in control.

I sighed and thought, *Thank you, God, that she's through that phase.* Yet something about the way she looked at me said it wasn't that simple.

"What's wrong?" I asked.

"I'm going to start going to another church," she said matter-of-factly. She wasn't arguing or asking permission. She had made up her mind and was telling me her decision. "Maybe we made the wrong decision in getting married," she said. "You're more concerned about other people's ingrown toenails than about your wife who is about to have a baby."

Her words shocked me. I now realize that was the only way I was going to get the message. Unfortunately, my first thought wasn't guilt for neglecting her or concern about how to change. My first thought was how it would look if my wife went to a different church. The parsonage was attached to the back of the church, so we shared the same parking lot.

This is going to be terrible, I thought. *Members will be driving to the church while Brenda is driving away from church. How is this going to make me look?*

"I'm about God's work. Don't you understand I have God's call on my life? Can't you support me in the ministry?"

"Can't you support me as a new mother and wife?"

"I am supporting you—"

"No, you're not. Everyone in the church is more important than me."

I insisted it wasn't true and that Brenda was the most important person in my life.

"No matter what you say, Sam, your actions show me something different. They're the ones you spend all your time with."

I finally had the sense to shut up and listen. I began to realize Brenda was seriously hurt. And I realized something even more important: I had failed her.

I couldn't sleep that night. I walked up to my office. It was about three o'clock Sunday morning. I was wrestling with myself and crying, "Lord, this doesn't make sense. The church is growing; the offerings have increased; people are being blessed. Yet my wife and I can't get along. She's saying she made the wrong decision in marrying me. What's going on? One part of my life is dying, and one part is growing."

When I was calm and ready to listen to God, I heard these words: "What shall it profit a man if he gain the whole world?" After a pause, I heard, "What shall it profit Sam if he gains the whole Full Gospel Assembly and loses his own family?"

It would be wonderful if I could report to you that that was a turning point in my life. Sadly, it wasn't that drastic, but it was a strong realization that I needed to slow down.

Brenda didn't go to another church. We talked and prayed together, and I began to get my priorities straight. But it was like watching a semitractor-trailer make a wide turn; it took a while for it to happen.

The fourth chapter also took place while I was the pastor of Full Gospel Assembly in Hartford. When I arrived, the church agreed to pay me $125 a week before taxes. It was not a lot of money, but we felt we could get by. When Rachel was born, we learned she was allergic to her mother's milk. We had to put her on a soy-based milk. That was a big expense we hadn't anticipated.

By the end of our third month in Hartford, we knew we couldn't keep on, because we couldn't even pay our bills. We didn't tell Brenda's parents or mine because we believed that God would provide for us. But nothing changed.

Finally, after several lengthy discussions, Brenda and I decided to go to the Social Services Office to apply for food stamps; I wasn't going to let Brenda and Rachel go hungry. When we walked inside their offices, I felt the terrible humiliation of having to ask for help.

It didn't feel any better as we filled out forms and told them everything about our lives. Then we waited. We sat in the foyer watching people come and go, and each minute I felt lower and less worthy. Finally someone called our name and sent us into the back where we would talk to a caseworker.

Then I faced even more embarrassment: the caseworker was a prominent member of the community.

This is quite a picture, I thought. *I'm the pastor, and I'm sitting across the desk from a member of the community asking her to approve me for food stamps.* To her credit, she didn't say anything to make me feel any more humiliated.

After the woman did all the tabulations, she looked up at me and said with sadness in her voice, "I'm sorry, but we can't approve you." Before I could ask why, she said, "You make $22 a week too much to receive food stamps."

I have no idea what I said to her. I just wanted out of there. It had been humiliating to apply and even worse to have to pour out our problems to a church member and discuss all our financial difficulties. And then, after all of that, we still didn't get approved. I couldn't even look her in the eyes as we shook hands and said goodbye.

Although we had only about a quarter of a mile to drive, it felt like the longest ride I had ever taken. We had humiliated ourselves and laid ourselves open to the whole town of Hartford. And we had been there long enough to know that in a small town, people talk. I thought about going to the church board and saying, "Cut my salary so I can get some help." And yet I didn't want them to know. I couldn't provide for my family—it was even worse than it had been in Gresham, Oregon. Then I bore the shame of a wife who brought in money. Now, even with my salary, I still couldn't support a family.

Somehow we made it, and we never told anyone else about our needs. Eventually the church gave me a raise in pay, and Rachel finally went off the soy milk.

My fifth chapter follows while we still lived in Hartford. We had exciting growth in the church. We went from 30 to 60 and quickly to 120. Offerings increased and the church paid all its bills. But what it cost me was too high of a price to pay, even though I didn't realize it. At first I was willing because I wanted the professional gratification of success. I loved to stand with my peers at church conferences and talk about my church growth.

In fact, the church had grown so much that we had to face a problem: Should we build a new church and turn our present sanctuary into a fellowship hall? The time seemed right. We had two groups in the church. The first represented those who had been there for years, and the second were those who had come to the church after I had become the pastor. I stood in the middle.

The older group saw me more as a chaplain who visited them in their homes and in the hospital, baptized believers, and performed weddings and funerals. To the newer group, I was a leader, and they were ready to follow whichever direction I led them to. We had a board, and it was technically their decision. But they knew, even as I knew, they would accept whatever I decided.

The old timers weren't in favor of building. They didn't particularly oppose it. They just didn't see much need for it. They wouldn't do anything outwardly if we went ahead, but I knew they'd grumble and complain to whomever would listen. The newer members were excited about growing and having larger facilities. They talked about it constantly. I loved their enthusiasm, and we even went to the extent of getting architectural plans. One day all the members of the board drove to different churches in the area to see what they had built.

Then I made the decision; I said "No." Looking back, I think it was a window of opportunity I totally missed. Within months after

I made the call, the church plateaued, and we never regained the growth momentum.

If there was blame, it was mine because I made the decision. I'd like to say it was a corporate decision, but I can't lie to myself. The board would have gone along either way. I took the simpler, easier way out. I didn't want to fight the passive-aggressive backlash of the older members. For a long time after that decision, I felt I had been a coward. I was hard on myself for not having the backbone to stand up to the problems a new building would cause, as well as the reaction from the older members.

At that time I couched my decision with worn phrases such as, "The Lord does everything in his own time. Maybe it's not the Lord's time for us to build." Looking back on it, I didn't want to pay the price it would cost me in human relationships. It was safer not to build. It would be easier to explain the decision to the new group, who trusted me at a higher level than the older group did.

Most of our life experiences can be summed up as successes or failures. Few qualify as neutral incidents. Our society, families, churches, educational institutions, and mentors instruct us on the secrets of success. But when was the last time someone shared insights on successful failure? There aren't many books, seminars, or discussion forums on the depressing topic. And yet I—like most people—have had more failures than successes.

I'm convinced that life isn't so much how we deal with success but how we respond to failure. Some people drive their life's vehicle and give greater attention to the rearview mirror than to the vistas of opportunity before them through the windshield.

Our destiny depends on this.

The worst thing about failure is simple: It's not getting up one more time, as you'll read elsewhere in this book. Many are still sitting where they fell and saying, "I could have made it if ... " or "If I would have only ..."

Judas betrayed Jesus; Peter denied our Lord. Both actions were failures. Yet the outcomes of their failures are on opposite ends. One got up again.

Judas realized his failure and chose not to get up. For him, that last failure was not an action but a permanent fact of his life. He saw no redeeming value in sincere repentance, in seeking a new direction. He viewed his whole life as a failure, and it drove him to suicide.

Peter also realized his failure but chose to get up. For him, failure was temporary. It was one action, not his whole life. Through repentance, he chose a radical direction. And that failure also drove him into the waiting arms of Jesus Christ.

There we have the difference between two of Jesus' disciples. One was consumed with hopelessness; the other found hope.

Two thousand years later, I have to face my own kind of failure. I've chosen the path of Peter. I refuse to see failure as ultimate. There is life after failure! The psalmist reminds us: "The steps of a good man are directed by the Lord. He delights in each step they take. If they fall it's not fatal, for the Lord holds them with his hand" (Psalm 37:23-24 tlb).

So get up. Get going. How you respond determines your destiny.

Remember, when you fall, God is holding your hand. He's waiting to pull you back to your feet.

Success is in the womb of failure.

Bishop Eddie L. Long
Senior Pastor, New Birth Missionary Church,
Decatur, Georgia

CHAPTER 2

Success: Born of Failure

BY BISHOP EDDIE L. LONG

I've failed many times. I'll fail many more times in the future. I've learned that failures aren't my entire life, but they're a necessary part of the journey to success.

"True success is born out of failure." I've heard that expression many times, and as I look back over my life, I can truly say, "Amen." This reminds me that God has used my failures to shape me into a vessel that he can use to accomplish specific tasks he has assigned to me.

Because I know that, I can say I'm not a vessel of failures, but a vessel of success, who is on assignment for God. I am a spoken word of God, and I must complete what he has assigned me to do.

"So shall my word be that goes forth from my mouth; it shall not return to me void, but it shall accomplish what I please, And it shall prosper in the thing for which I sent it" (Isa. 55:11 nkjv).

By going through many failures, I've learned three important lessons. When I operate with these three principles in mind, I can continue to focus on God and trust that God will make it happen.

I didn't know those principles the first day that I started to follow Jesus Christ. I had to learn them, and I learned them by failing.

First, God has called me. I don't want to give the impression that failing is easy to get over. It's painful, and sometimes it takes a long time to move past the pain. The worst part of failure is that it often makes us question our calling to fulfill the task God has given to us.

We, who are ministers, pastors, or workers for the gospel of Christ, have to face failure and not just once or twice but many, many times. Failure is part of our destiny; we can't escape it. Failure, however, isn't our grave; it's an opportunity for life. Failure isn't a conclusion but a beginning.

I can say those words now, but I couldn't always say them. I wasn't able to accept failure gracefully—not until God spoke in my spirit and made me know that I was called by him. That word brought assurance to me.

Reading in the Bible about some of the men and women chosen by God helps us to understand this. Many of them failed at their tasks in one way or another.

Genesis 20:1-18 tells us that Abraham was called to be the father of many nations. That was God's plan for him. But to save his own life, instead of trusting God to deliver him, Abraham chose to lie to the king of Gerar about Sarah being his wife. God still birthed many nations out of his genes and called him the father of faith. Why? That was Abraham's destiny, his calling—God was faithful.

Or what about Peter, the great apostle? Luke 22:54–62 records Peter's failure by denying Jesus. Yet in the Book of Acts, we see Peter preaching and thousands being saved. It's a story of failure that leads to triumph.

Both of these examples—and I could give you many others— remind us that God will take our failures and use them as our testimonies because we are strengthened afterward. Once we have failed and moved on, we're stronger and more faithful to God.

I'm no Abraham or Peter, but like everyone else, I've had several failures in my life. At the time, they seemed really bad. And they were. Yet as I look back, I realize they equipped me to be more sensitive to God's people.

Knowing that first principle, that God has called me, has taken me through the most painful times. For instance, I can remember working for a major corporation and doing things that other people were doing, but they were wrong to do. I got caught, and I knew

I wasn't pleasing my employer who paid me or God who loved me. They fired me because of my failure to comply with the rules of the company.

I really felt like a failure that day. "But everyone else does it," I kept saying. "Why didn't they get fired too?" I felt ashamed, and I couldn't stand the humiliation. I even got angry with God. "You did this to me. You should have protected me." In my hurt I felt God had let me down at the time when I really wanted to serve him.

I couldn't accept responsibility for my failure. Then I talked to the man who was my spiritual father. He wouldn't let me get away with crying, "But everyone else does it." "You aren't everyone else," he said. "You're a child of God, and you did wrong." Those were not the words I wanted to hear, but they were the words I needed to hear. He wouldn't allow me to have a private pity party. With his help, I began to admit I had failed. I asked God to forgive me, and I knew I was still useful for God's plan.

Another tragic time in my life involved my first marriage. I knew the ideal plan for marriage and how to be the perfect family for everyone to admire. We would have the little house with the white picket fence. After a hard day's work, I would come home to my lovely wife, beautiful children, and happy home. Yes, it was a dream—and not a very realistic one.

Within a matter of months my dream had turned into a nightmare. I was young in the ministry and trying to do the best I knew in the marriage. But the more I tried, the more our relationship seemed out of control.

"If my marriage fails," I heard myself say, "I can't be used effectively by God as a Christian minister." I believed I had to hold an already broken marriage together so that God would use me.

I talked to friends and to other pastors. Most of them said, "If your marriage fails, you can never be a pastor."

What was I to do? I knew God had called me to pastor, and yet my marriage was falling apart. Nothing I did seemed to make it any better. I was in terrible emotional pain. Everything I lived for seemed to be slipping away. Many times I wanted to give up. One thing, however, kept me focused. God had called me to pastor. I knew that and never once doubted it.

"How can I be a pastor?" I cried out to God. I didn't know what to do. But slowly I came to accept that I could trust God to work it out. God had called me. Now it was up to God to fulfill the calling in my life.

It wasn't easy. After my marriage failed, I felt devastated for a long time. "How can I help others when I can't help myself?" I prayed. "How can I advise people when I can't solve my own problems?"

I also realized something. I couldn't solve their problems, but I could understand them. I knew pain. I had hurt, and I had survived. I had turned to Jesus, and he had lifted my distress and discouragement. That's how I could help. I could be sensitive to their needs and care about their suffering.

Now I look back and thank God for what I learned from those painful experiences of a doomed marriage and divorce. That failure prepared me to be a better pastor. I learned, through the failure of a relationship, to remain focused on God no matter how unpleasant the situation. Remaining focused on the one who called me is my way of saying, "I know it was God who got me through this time of failure."

Second, God has chosen the road I'm on. This is another truth I've learned to accept in my life. I now understand that the road of destiny is sometimes filled with failure and challenges. It's no accident that I am where I am today. I am right here, exactly in this place, because this is the path God wants me on. As long as I stay on the right road—the one God has chosen for me—I'll still fail sometimes, but I won't turn back or leave the right road. Even in the midst of my failure I'm making progress. By the grace of God, I am going forward.

Third, I will accomplish my assignment because God will empower me. After I failed many times, I finally figured it out. Despite my failures, God had not given up on me. I made up my mind that from then on I would trust God no matter what happened.

"With God's help," I said, "I'm going to get up after each failure and move on." Through my failures, I have come to believe that God has ordered my footsteps. There are some lessons I don't seem able to learn except by falling flat on my face first. I'm not saying God authors my failures, but he uses them to bring me closer to him.

"True success is born out of failure." I believe those words.

I believe them because I have lived them.

Rev. Wiley Jackson, Jr.
Senior Pastor, Gospel Tabernacle, Atlanta, Georgia

Failure: The Backdoor to Blessing

BY REV. WILEY JACKSON, JR.

My career as a pastor started with a lot of enthusiasm, but I had the wrong vision.

In late 1982, I was sitting on my bed at home and watching a famous evangelist on television. At the time, I was a frustrated church member. As I watched, I said, "I can do better than that on my off days."

Just then God spoke to me. "You have one problem, Wiley. He's preaching and you're sitting here on your bed."

Those words stirred me into action. The next week I started looking until I found a storefront. I rented it even though I didn't have a single member or knew anyone who would come to the church. But I felt I had to do it because I had a strong desire in my spirit to build a church for God.

A lot of people asked me, "Did God tell you to go to that particular store front?"

"No. I rented it," I answered them, "because it was the cheapest place I could find." It was located at the Parkview Plaza Shopping Center in Southeast Atlanta and cost me $250 a month. For $300, I could pay the rent as well as the light bill and the gas. I worked for

Frito Lay, so I knew I could swing that much money. On top of the monthly payments, I borrowed $1,500 so I could put in seats and a small pulpit.

I began to preach at what I then called the Gospel Tabernacle Deliverance Center and trusted God that the people would come in. And they did—one by one.

When I began it was frightening. I had no one by my side. I had a lot of friends who thought they helped by telling me what they believed was best for me. "It's not the will of God," was the advice most often.

More than one looked at me and said, "You've got to be crazy."

Starting a church was a big undertaking. Finally, I said, "Well, Lord, if it doesn't work, I can always continue with my job."

From the first day it was exciting. I loved to preach about Jesus Christ, even if nobody came to listen. What a joy it was when people did listen. By the end of the first year I had twelve members. Twelve whole members. Five of them were from my family, but they were members. I hadn't become a big-time pastor, but I was doing God's will, and it was exciting.

I did just about everything in those days. For instance, sometimes the whole church went on trips to sing and preach. We could put all our members into one van, and I'd drive. Once we got to our destination, I'd check all the equipment, set it up, and then run into a back room, change clothes, and preach the sermon. After the sermon was over I'd change clothes again, take down the equipment, put it into the van, and drive the people back home. A lot of work, but I loved it.

I didn't complain because I was too thrilled about what God was doing. It may not sound like much to some people, but with those twelve members, I felt I had become a success in the ministry. I also knew it was just the beginning. By the end of the second year, we had twenty-four members.

Now I was finally a big-time pastor. We needed two vans to carry all the church members. We were growing, and I had visions of fifty, a hundred, even two hundred people worshiping together.

It didn't work that way. I can think of two major reasons I didn't progress after that. First, I still had a lot of doubts about God calling me to be a pastor. Maybe it was because I wanted to preach so badly and didn't have the needed confidence. But I struggled with that question for a long time.

My second problem was that I didn't know how to exercise leadership. Rather than taking responsibility and asserting myself, I often put off making a decision or let someone else do it. One time I said to the members, "I believe God is telling us to buy another van." But I didn't know how to proceed, so I asked, "What do you have to say?"

"We don't need another van," somebody complained.

"You're probably right," I said. "It's not time to buy a van." I knew in my spirit that God was telling me to do it. But I gave in to the negative voices and failed to exercise leadership.

Near the end of the second year, we had a church split. I lost twelve of the members—twelve of the good-paying members—and it cut our membership in half. I felt like David in the days when he ran from King Saul, left with only those who were in debt, distress, or discontented.

After the twelve members left, I went home totally depressed. I wasn't married at that time, so I really was alone. I had failed God, the people, and myself. I cried out, "God, I didn't ask for this in the first place. I've still got a good job. I'll just go to work and forget this church idea."

I told myself I'd never go back to the Gospel Tabernacle. I'd never be a preacher again. It had been stupid to think I could lead a growing church. Yet even as I told God those things, I knew I wanted to preach more than anything else.

The next day, my father, who wasn't saved at that time, came to see me. "I heard what happened to you."

"I don't want to talk about it. You don't understand church business—"

"I may not understand church business, Son, but I know one thing, and you need to know it too. You are the pastor. No matter what goes on in that church, you are responsible."

"I don't want to hear that. I'm not responsible. They did me wrong. They lied and betrayed me. They let me down. I didn't ask for this."

"Yeah, I know," he said, "but you're still responsible. If you work at it, you can continue, Son."

He talked some more, even though I didn't like what he said. After he left, I kept thinking about his words. No matter how I tried, I couldn't get away from what he had said. Then I realized something

I'd never forget: the people who left weren't to blame. My father was right; I had denied my responsibility. I hadn't led them, so one of the deacons had done what I wouldn't do. He took the leadership role on just about everything. When he left, they followed their leader.

It took a while, but God used those words from my dad to turn me around. If I didn't lead, someone else would. I decided I had to go back to the storefront church and take responsibility for the ministry God had called me to.

"I can do it," I said, with a confidence I had never felt before.

From that bad experience I learned that it's important for a pastor or anybody thinking about going into the ministry to be assured of the call. When they're assured of the call, they can assume leadership, and they can trust God. During those first two years, I hadn't had the assurance I needed. I got it only after losing those twelve members.

Before the church split, my younger brother, Rodney, had come into the church. Even though he was capable, I didn't want him as the assistant pastor because he was my brother. I didn't want people to say, "The only reason Rodney is the assistant pastor is because he's Wiley's brother." To avoid that, I tried other men, but they never worked out. When I started over, I decided that as soon as I needed an assistant, Rodney would be the one.

God told me to go back to the church and have a Praise-a-thon, and I said, "Yes, Lord." This time I didn't ask anyone's opinion; this time I told them what God had told me.

"This is what we're going to do. For the next thirty days, I'm going to minister on only one thing: praising the Lord," I said as I looked right at them. "I'm not going to talk about the people who left. I'm not going to talk about how bad they were. I'm only going to talk about Jesus and how good he is!"

"Praise the Lord," was the first comment I heard.

I began to lead the people; we praised the Lord every day and in everything. Even with all the praising, things didn't miraculously turn around. In fact, we faced terrible problems. The church roof began to leak. We praised the Lord for giving us a building while we worked hard to raise the money to repair it. The van broke down, and for a long time we didn't have the money to have it fixed. We praised the Lord that we had a van at all and praised him for the next one we were going to buy.

By the end of those thirty days, we had started the church's third year. I had exercised leadership, I had done what God told me to do, and God honored my obedience. I couldn't believe how quickly the situation turned around. God started sending new people to the church.

"How did you hear about the church?" we asked the new people.

"I really don't know," was the way the answer usually started. One woman said, "I just got off the bus out on Memorial Drive and saw there was a church here in the shopping center."

"Somebody told me about this church," one man said. "I don't know who the guy was. He said he didn't go to your church, but it was a good one, and he thought I'd like it here."

Our church was located in the middle of a shopping center on a busy Atlanta street. On one side of us was a bingo parlor and on the other was the Mellow Fellow Nightclub. Sometimes I'd be preaching and I'd hear, "B-5," followed by a loud yell, "Bingo!" in the middle of my message.

On the other side of our church was the nightclub. They would start playing rhythm and blues music. Many of us had come out of that lifestyle, but we still remembered the music. It was hard for me to stand in my pulpit and try to preach when I'd hear one of my favorite R&B songs through the walls.

The members would try to listen to me, but all the time, they were patting their feet in time to the music. "Praise the Lord," I'd cry out and hope God would distract them from the music.

Despite things like that, God continued to bring in new people. So many came I needed an assistant, and I knew God wanted Rodney. (After Rodney became the assistant pastor, he went to Beulah Heights Bible College, graduated, and went on to the Interdenominational Theological Center for his master's degree in theology. He now teaches at Beulah Heights. In 1997, the students and faculty voted him Teacher of the Year.)

The more I exercised leadership, the more the ministry grew. One day in 1985, I had a vision. I saw a church building. It just floated down out of the sky. It was a real vision, not just a thought. The doors opened, and it was as if a camera panned the sanctuary while it went through the doors. I could see everything that was happening. I saw myself preaching in the pulpit, and the place was full of people listening and praising God.

"Oh, Lord, that can't be me." I think I was too overwhelmed at first to believe that could be me with that kind of church.

Yet I knew it was God. In fact, I was so sure, I talked to an architect that same week and told him what I had seen. He worked with me and drew up plans to build the kind of church building I had seen in the vision.

I went back and told our members, "We're going to build a new church." At the time we had only seventy-five members, but I felt like a full-blown, national pastor and big-time evangelist. My dreams were large, and they were all going to happen right away.

I had received a vision and just rushed right into it, but I didn't do any research on the building costs. "We're going to build this huge church," I told the members, "and I believe it will cost us two hundred thousand dollars. God said we could raise two hundred thousand dollars to build it."

By now they were used to my exercising leadership, and no one argued.

A few weeks later, I brought in a bonding company to handle the financing of the church. We would have to raise the money by selling bonds for them to loan us the money to pay for the construction. The bonding company and the lenders earned interest, so it was like working with a bank, except that we had to sell the bonds ourselves.

From then on, at every service I said, "God says as soon as we get two hundred thousand dollars, we can build." I didn't even have the final plans; I just had a picture in my mind. I figured that the money we raised would get a building up. After we got inside to worship, we could finish the rest of it ourselves.

We continued to pray and raise money. No matter how hard we worked, it seemed as if we could never raise the two hundred thousand dollars. Something always happened. Once, the roof started to leak, and we couldn't sit there with water dripping in. We had to fix the hole in the roof.

Despite all the setbacks, I didn't get discouraged. "These walls must fall," I'd say. "We're going to conquer the devil! This is the will of God, and we're going to make it happen!"

We didn't make it happen. Time ran out for us to raise the money for the bond program. We had the land in our name—even though it wasn't paid for—but that's about all we had.

I had failed again. Depression and self-pity hit me. "What's wrong with me?" I asked God. "I tried to lead, and I led to failure." I knew I had to get up in front of those people and say, "I missed God this time."

It was difficult, but I did it. I had to. "This just isn't the Lord's will." I said. "I believe it is God's will for us to build, but I didn't have the timing right. I got off on the wrong vision about building the church. You know, a lot of times God is talking to you and a lot of other voices are talking to you. The devil talks to you. And God is talking too."

"How do we know when it's God's voice?" one of the members asked.

"It's like choosing doors. You open door number one, and it's not right. So you close it and put an X on it, and you know not to go back to door number one anymore." I paused and knew I had to tell them I had failed.

"Through the process of elimination is how we know what's right. I've been checking those doors, and I found the two-hundred-thousand-dollar door and opened it, but it wasn't the right one." Again I paused and looked at them before I added, "I'll never listen to that voice again. I put an X on that door. But there is a right door in God. And when we open it, everything will go just like God said."

As I continued to preach that morning, I told them they needed to understand that I was only a human being, a man God uses. "However, I am also a man that misses God on various issues." Then I told them plainly that I had missed God.

"Whew, Pastor, I'm glad you said that," said one of the men. "For a while we were thinking you weren't like us."

They understood. They forgave me, and I felt their love. My failing at choosing that bond program helped me to realize that I'm not God. I often tell my people that when we start acting like God, we take on Godlike problems. Nobody can handle Godlike problems but God himself. When we are under God, then it's up to him to handle the Godlike problems.

That experience of failure changed my ministry. Since then, one policy I have put in place with Gospel Tabernacle is that whenever something happens right or wrong, the pastor will get up and address it. I will tell them what I did, and what happened, and what we're going to do about it.

To my amazement, when the people accepted that I had failed, it didn't affect my leadership. I told them I still believed it was God's will for us to build, but it would happen in God's way and with God's timing.

Then I backtracked to do things right. First, I had plans drawn up for the church. We raised twenty-four thousand to pay the architect for them. We didn't have money to build, but we made ourselves ready for God's timing. We talked to different companies about constructing a building, even though we still didn't have money.

I went to every bank in Atlanta and asked for a loan for one million dollars—the true cost to build what I had seen in my vision. Without exception, they turned me down.

At the last bank I sat down to talk to the loan officer. He wasn't very friendly to begin with. Then when I showed him our financial records, he shook his head. "Do you mean to tell me you think you can borrow this much money to build a church with these finances?"

He could have turned us down nicely the way the others had, but he was just plain mean. I left with my feelings hurt.

"They've all turned us down," I said to Rodney with tears in my eyes, "but I believe someone in the United States of America is going to lend us the money to build a church."

Both of us knew it wouldn't be a bank in Atlanta.

A construction firm in Greenville, South Carolina advertised in *Pulpit Helps* magazine. "We build churches," the ad read. At that time, Rodney worked for Eastern Airlines and had a family pass, so we could fly free. Rodney and I flew up to see them.

In the middle of showing our plans, the headman said, "There's a company in Alabama that provides money for congregations to build churches. We usually charge twenty thousand dollars for this information but there's something about you guys I like, so I'm telling it to you free."

We had just met him, and we believed it was God that made him come forth with that information. He explained that the company helped churches through a bond issue, but this one was different. The company itself sold all the bonds.

Rodney and I flew straight from Greenville to Alabama. When we got there the man was too busy to talk to us, but he did say we could see him in Atlanta the following week. His company had a representative in Atlanta that he was going to meet with. As it turned out, an emergency came up so that I couldn't meet with him and neither could Rodney. Our church's administrator, Melvin Drake, went to meet him.

We didn't know it then, but the Atlanta representative had once worked for Melvin and liked him. That man set up a meeting with one of the vice presidents of the company. We took our financial information to him and said, "We want to borrow a million dollars for the church."

We knew our financial statement didn't stand up to our paying back a million dollars. He looked it over. Then he said, "Yes, Pastor Jackson, you can do it. We can get you the money, and you can build the church. Will sixty days be okay?"

"Sixty days would be fine," I said, so overwhelmed I could hardly get the words out. "That's just right on schedule."

Rodney and I have often said that for those sixty days, that man and his family were as safe as they'd ever be in their lives because we prayed for them fervently every day and fasted regularly. "Lord, don't let him have an accident," we prayed. "Don't let him even get sick. Don't let anything bad happen to him before we get our money."

As excited as I was, I kept thinking, it can't be this easy. Something will happen to make it fail.

The company sent the money.

Rodney and I went to the very bank where the man had hurt my feelings. "I hope you remember me," I said. "You turned us down when we wanted to borrow money. Today I'm here because we want to open a checking account."

"Oh, yes, yes, I do remember you." He looked at me in a sarcastic way, and I knew he was thinking, *Oh, you're back again.* "How much you want to deposit to open the account?"

"One million dollars."

He stared at me and then at the check I held in my hand. "Oh, yes, Reverend Jackson, we can help you!" He gave me the biggest smile he was capable of. "Just sit right down here." He pointed to chairs for us to sit in. "Yes, just sit down, and we'll fill out the papers."

He opened the account and gave me a temporary checkbook. When I got up, he extended his hand. "So good to do business with you, Reverend Jackson."

I took his hand, shook it, and said, "Sir, never mess with a child of God."

He smiled sheepishly, and I knew I had made my point. Since then, whenever I see him, I go out of my way to talk to him. He'll always respond, "Reverend, whatever you say is all right."

It took us a full year, but we built Gospel Tabernacle, and as we like to say, "The rest is his story."

When we started to build, we still had seventy-five members and met for another year in that tiny building. We experienced no growth during that time. Doubts would start to come, but I'd remind myself that God had provided the money, and God would do whatever it took to fill up the new building.

We moved into the church in 1988. Immediately the growth began. Now, ten years later, we hold two services and see fifteen hundred members every Sunday.

It took nearly seven years to pay off the million dollars. Since that time we've enlarged and redone some things. Right now we're getting ready for another two million-dollar addition to this church.

Despite my failures, God had given me a vision, and God fulfilled the vision.

Dr. David C. Cooper
Senior Pastor, Mount Paran Church of God,
Atlanta, Georgia

CHAPTER 4

Failure: Paying the Price for Growth

BY DR. DAVID C. COOPER

If I had asked the members of our church in Athens, "Do you want to grow?" everybody would have said, "Yes!" If I had asked, "Do you want to change?" they would probably have said, "No."

The concepts are synonymous. Growth involves change. As a church we wanted to grow and reach our community for Christ. I articulated that message regularly from the pulpit, and everyone rallied around the call. The paradox was that although they wanted to grow, they also wanted to stay in the comfort zone. Growth isn't comfortable.

Because I was starting off in the ministry, I didn't always know how to handle change. Passion and determination are my greatest strengths; people seem to feed off those qualities. Of course, they're also my weaknesses, which I have to struggle with from time to time. As a determined leader, I had the tendency to take the ball and run with it without taking time to make sure my team was following.

When Barbie and I moved to Living Faith Fellowship in Athens in 1981, God gave me a vision for the city and the ministry he was raising up. I felt a deep passion about what God was doing in our midst and challenged the church to stretch and to change. Even though my proposals demanded change, the people respected me for my vision enough to go along with them.

That was the situation in October 1981, when I was twenty-five years old. My wife, Barbie, and I went to our first church, in Athens, Georgia. The church had been started about eighteen months earlier in a metal building on one acre of land that had previously housed a gymnastic center.

Even though the attendance had risen to forty, the pastor had become discouraged. One Sunday morning in March 1981, the members found the pastor's resignation attached to the front door.

When we arrived six months later there were only twelve people who had held on—twelve people and no money. The church carried three separate mortgages for furniture, fixtures, and the original building. Most of the payments came out of the members' personal savings. They were discouraged, but I went there because, by faith, I saw the potential.

By May of 1982, our morning attendance had broken the one hundred barrier. That was faster growth than I had expected. Every Sunday we had first-time visitors, and most stayed.

We continued to grow. For each of the ten years I stayed in Athens, the church annually assimilated an average of more than one hundred members—the net gain after subtracting those who moved away. The church also grew in its diversity, with good representations of every age group from children to senior citizens and college students to families. By the time I left, we had a multiple pastoral staff to oversee these areas of ministry, producing a balanced church.

———— ✦ ————

Growth also produces challenges.

One challenge in particular involved choir robes. After three years of ministry, we were averaging more than three hundred people in our morning worship service.

After we hired Terry Ross, a full-time music minister, I suggested that we purchase choir robes. He agreed.

We talked with the choir leadership and purchased the robes. However, the choir was under the impression that they would wear them only for special occasions. Many of them had come out of churches steeped in certain traditions that they associated with spiritual deadness. Some of them believed that if they wore choir robes, it meant our church was going backward, moving into formality, and that we would quench the Holy Spirit.

Terry appeased them by saying the robes were for Easter Sunday, which was true. Everybody was all right with that one-time event. The choir looked great that morning and people told them so.

After the service Terry and I agreed that the choir should wear the robes every Sunday. The positive feedback from the congregation regarding the appearance of the choir, along with the fact that the Holy Spirit moved mightily during the Easter morning services, was enough to convince them that the choir robes wouldn't hinder the work of the Holy Spirit.

Unfortunately, that wasn't the end of the issue of robes. Aaron, one of our finest members, came to my home one day. "I've got to talk to you," he said. "I don't sense the Holy Spirit at work in the church like I did at the beginning." That's a strong statement for a pastor to hear.

Immediately I wondered, *Where have I failed? What did I do wrong?* Sometimes my need to be affirmed clouded my objective judgment because I wanted people to like me. But I pushed my confusion aside and asked Aaron, "What do you mean?"

"I can't put my hand on it exactly, but I feel we used to have closer fellowship and were more open to the Holy Spirit in our worship."

I kept probing until I got down to the real issue that was bothering him.

"The choir robes symbolize formalism and traditionalism," he said. "By having them, we're moving away from the freedom of the Spirit."

By probing a little further, I realized the real problem was the rapid growth of the congregation. He had come to the church in the early days when we had about fifty members and now we had grown to over three hundred. When we had the smaller membership, I could minister directly to him. Aaron had had a lot of problems before committing his life to Christ. I was able to give him personal help. As the size of the membership grew, however, he felt he was losing that close connection with me.

After we talked about his feelings I assured him that I would make a concerted effort to do as much for him and with him as I could, but I added, "I need you to understand the limitations of my schedule. I enjoyed the church when we had only fifty members too. I loved the close fellowship we had. But now we've grown, and not only is the church having to sacrifice its time with me, I'm having to sacrifice my time as well. That's part of the price of growth."

Once Aaron understood that I couldn't spend as much time with him and the others as I had in the past, our relationship was back on track. I was paying the same price as he and the others were paying. He seemed then to understand the need to change and pledged his support to me.

By 1988, the sanctuary was inadequate to hold the crowd, so we started an 8:30 morning service. After having the early service for a year or so—and the attendance continued to grow in both services—one of the elders said he needed to talk to me.

"I'm concerned about the two services," he said.

When I asked about his concern, he said, "I feel as if we have two churches now. We used to be one family, but now the people that come at 8:30 don't know the people at 11:00 and the people that come at 11:00 don't know the people that come at 8:30. I don't get to see the people I used to see."

"That's the price of growth," I said. "But let me ask you a question. When you come at 11:00 do you know everyone in the service?"

"Why, no, of course not."

"Then what difference does it make if you don't know everybody in the 8:30 service? You don't know everybody as it is." I explained that we weren't trying to make sure everyone knew everybody else in the services. I pointed him back to our mission and purpose and asked, "What did Jesus commission us to do?"

"To go into all the world and make disciples."

"Exactly. And if we're going to do that, it has a price tag—we won't know everyone in the church. We've grown so much now you don't know everyone anyway. We could add four services and it wouldn't make any difference, would it?"

"I see what you mean." The light had come on inside his head, and he never offered another word of objection about the two-service model of worship.

After we reached the 350 mark, we pressed toward 500. It was time to make a change in the administration of the church. The elders still counted the money from offerings, deposited it, and had oversight of expenditures. Everything was under their control. I proposed two things. First, that we move Terry Ross from music to business administration since he had a background in business. Second, that we hire an independent auditing service to give us the best record-keeping system to protect ourselves in any kind of liability issue. The auditing service would also provide the best financial management package for the church.

New struggles began. Two of the elders, John and Shawn, didn't like my plans, even though neither said, "We won't do this." At the time we had seven elders and we went to the mountains for a retreat. Until we started to talk about the administrative program, I didn't realize what a big struggle it was for them to give up direct management of the finances or how strongly the two men felt. Since John was very involved with the finances, he saw it as a kind of demotion.

The idea of making Terry the business administrator upset them the most. I knew they would resist, but I didn't realize they would react so strongly. Even though they didn't say it, I knew the reason they resisted: they were losing their position.

It was apparent to me that John and Shawn needed some special attention if we were going to work through their objections. So I rode back to Athens from the retreat with them. That gave me two hours to talk through their concerns, just the three of us. They both admitted that the size of our budget warranted a full-time administrator. They were also supportive when they realized that they wouldn't be cut out of the loop. The administrator would be fully accountable to the elders.

The lesson I learned through that experience is how difficult it is for people established in congregations to give up control and position.

At the time we were making the change in our administration, there were two other significant things going on. First was the matter of the church's tax exemption as a nonprofit corporation. When the church started in 1979, the trustees filed for a State of Georgia charter. But the State failed to inform them of the need to also file with the federal government to become tax exempt. They assumed that was automatic. As a result the church had operated without tax exemption for seven years and didn't know it.

After we hired the accounting firm, the first thing they did was to conduct a full inventory of everything. They also discovered this oversight and our vulnerable position.

That could have meant that contributions given for the previous seven years were not exempt for tax purposes. I talked to the elders to help them understand the seriousness of the situation.

The biggest reason this troubled us was because of a major contribution given by one of our members who had been fired from the University of Georgia because she refused to give star football players passing grades they didn't earn. She sued and won a large financial settlement. *People Magazine* quoted her as saying, "I'm going to tithe to my church, Living Faith Fellowship."

In all likelihood her contribution would be audited. If so the IRS would have found that our church was without tax exemption at that time.

While we were going through the process of securing exemption status, I proposed that the elders appoint Terry administrator. From that experience I learned that in a growing church, the people who have control have to be willing to let go of it. Like anyone else, once they had something, they didn't want to surrender it.

The next eighteen months was a long, painful period for me as the process dragged on. My stomach felt as if it were tied into knots. But I felt tied in knots just as much because the elders dragged their heels. They kept asking, "How do we know we can trust the system? If Terry's managing the money, how can we know it's being managed right?" (This happened during the time of Jimmy Bakker and the PTL scandal, which created a nationwide sense of mistrust of all preachers and church leaders.)

During one meeting I laid it out for them rather bluntly. "We adopt an annual budget that allows *X* number of dollars for each area of the ministry. The monthly financial statement shows the balance of all receipts and expenditures. The administrator manages the money only with purchase orders that we've approved in the budget. He accounts for every dime." I also pointed out that every month they would get a statement from an independent auditing firm that tracked every dollar given and spent. They finally agreed.

As promised, they got monthly statements. Terry also had a few men from the church work with him as a subcommittee, and that helped to build trust in the new system. The elders soon felt more secure and had a stronger sense of confidence.

I recall sitting in an elders' meeting on one occasion. Terry was going over the financial statement, and a couple of elders brought up minor issues—again the issue of trust—and I got upset. They actually had more financial accountability and disclosure than they had had before, but some of them couldn't see it.

After listening to all I wanted to hear, I said, "Just let the man do his job! The elders can't account for every single expenditure the church makes. We approve the budget. He does his job by keeping the budget balanced."

Amazingly, they all smiled at my response. They had finally gotten the point. Our relationships were strong enough to handle such self-disclosure, a quality of the eldership for which I was thankful.

I'm glad I had a good relationship with those men because we could be honest with each other. Even so it still took about eighteen months for everybody to get on board and feel good about the changes in administration.

About that time, the IRS admitted that they had been negligent and didn't give the right information when the church was originally organized. They gave us tax exempt status and made it retroactive to the time of the foundation of the corporation.

What a day of relief it was when the issue was finally resolved.

During 1989, the church assimilated over two hundred new members, and our receipts grew more than $200,000. When I left after ten years, the budget that had slid to the verge of bankruptcy in 1981 had now risen to a million and a half dollars a year. At last we had the administrative infrastructure in place to handle that increase, but the changes had come through painful transitions.

From my experience with the elders I learned the importance of personal time with my leaders. It took countless hours, but I needed to be available to them. Sometimes after elders' meetings I'd stand outside and talk with them. When I realized they didn't understand something we had done in the meeting, I'd say, "Here's what we're doing and here's why." The personal attention was important, and it bonded us.

Despite differences of opinion, I never thought I would lose any of them because we had built solid relationships. At the leadership level in our church, we stressed that we wanted to be gut-level honest. We all learned that if someone got angry or showed their bad side, the others wouldn't hold it against him.

Our relationship to each other and God was strong enough that we could accept those occasional outbursts and differences. We determined to learn and to grow together.

There were times I had to submit to their counsel, even when I disagreed. For instance, by the time we had 250 attending, we still had a gravel parking lot. We already owned one acre, and then we bought two more adjacent acres for parking. We had $350,000 in the annual budget and a gravel parking lot! I could see what gravel did to women's high heels. I wanted to borrow the money to asphalt it, but the elders said "No." I let them know how I felt, but they still didn't think we should borrow the money.

I yielded to their counsel. So we delayed until we raised the money through special offerings.

All these stories, while seemingly insignificant, underscore the paradox of the growing church—everyone wants the church to grow, but few are willing to pay the price for that growth. No matter how we look at it, growth means change, and change is uncomfortable for everyone.

Through the years of pastoral ministry, I've learned that every pastor and congregation will make a number of mistakes while they try to grow their ministry. Failure, however, doesn't have to be final. Failures and blunders can enable us to grow in the image of Christ and to learn invaluable lessons about ministry. From time to time, I remind myself that the only people who never make mistakes are those who never try to accomplish anything.

As Winston Churchill observed, "Success is going from one failure to another without losing your enthusiasm."

Rev. Collette L. Gunby
Senior Pastor, Green Pastures Christian
Ministries, Inc., Decatur, Georgia

CHAPTER 5

First Comes Failure

BY REV. COLLETTE L. GUNBY

Green Pastures Christian Ministries, Inc. was birthed from the failed lives of Ronald and Colette Gunby. Failure came to the marriage of a church girl. I didn't comprehend the God that I served until tragedy hit and everything around me began to collapse. My Cinderella, happily-ever-after life was having multiple crises.

Father's Day June 16, 1974 started peacefully. We had two beautiful children, Kelley (5 years old) and Douglas (4 months old). Two months earlier we had faced the sudden loss of Ronald's father. Neither of us had been prepared to face that loss.

Ronald's mom wanted him to go with her to place flowers on his dad's grave. He appeared reluctant, so I tried to get him to obey his mom's wish and go with her to the cemetery. Ronald was still grieving and angry over the loss of his father and didn't want to go to the grave. Looking back, I now realize that he didn't know where to place his hurt and loss. I didn't know how to help him. We began to argue and yell at each other. This went on for perhaps an hour. We finally stopped yelling, but the matter wasn't settled.

Since it was Father's Day, Ronald, still angry, finally drove me to my dad's house. We argued all the way. He put us out of the car and drove away. Ronald was to sing with the church choir that evening. When he got back home and started to dress, his shirt was not ironed, so he called me and yelled at me. Nothing I said satisfied him. One word led to another. He told me he was coming over. I knew deep within that this was a man in an uncontrolled rage. Everyone in the house felt the tension in my voice and saw the concern on my face.

That wasn't the first time Ronald had displayed anger in front of my family. It was just as if everyone was on alert. Before Ronald got to the house, I called the Atlanta Police Department three or four times. They never came.

When Ronald arrived, my dad met him at the door and began to talk to him as a father would talk to a son. His efforts to defuse the anger enraged Ronald all the more.

Finally, all of us went outside, and I hoped he would leave there peacefully.

My five-year-old daughter, Kelley, and I were only a few feet away watching as Ronald, with our infant son in his arms, reached for the gun that he had stuck in the back of his pants. Before he could get the gun out, my father, who always carried a gun, shot Ronald three times with his .38 caliber gun.

I stared at them and heard the gunfire. As I screamed, I saw my husband falling in slow motion to the ground. At first, I didn't know if he was dead or alive. Our son seemed to fall slowly by some invisible force to the concrete sidewalk and lay there unhurt. The next few moments felt like an eternity. I heard music, not earthly, but like a big page was turning in a Heavenly Book, as if it signified an ending of a chapter.

I picked up my son, frantically praying that he had not been shot. Thank God, when I examined my son I found no bullet wounds. There was not a scratch on him. Kelley was unhurt as well.

Someone came and took her into the house next door. I sighed and thanked God that the children were both physically all right.

Then I stared at Ronald, unable to believe what had happened.

We had started out that day as normal people. "God, where are you?" I cried. "How did this happen? Why did the pain and anger have to get to this point?" Everything blurred at that time.

I looked up and saw helicopters flying around and police cars parked in front of my father's house. Guns pointed at all of us. Over a loud speaker from the helicopter, a voice yelled, "Hold your hands up, and don't move."

Our lives had changed forever.

Doctors operated on Ronald for eight hours in the front, flipped him over, and operated on him for another eight hours in the back. He died on the operating table, and the Lord brought him back to life. I believed then and still believe that the breath God breathed into him that day was his second chance. He remained in a coma for several days before he responded.

Yes, Ronald would live, but he'd never walk again. He was paralyzed from the waist down. I thought that after he survived the shooting he would change, realizing the wrong he had done. He did change—for the worse.

"How did we get here?" I cried out to God. "We are good people. What did we do so wrong to get here?" Those questions stayed in my mind, and I couldn't get rid of them. My life had fallen apart. I looked for somebody to give me all the right answers. Somehow I knew that nobody could help me but God. I knew that we were in a place that human understanding could not fathom.

I've never felt any animosity toward my daddy. I believe he did what any true man would do to protect his home and defend himself against my husband's angry rage. Yet it saddened me that the two most precious men in my life had pulled guns on each other.

Never had I felt at such a low point in my life. No human being could give me what I needed to satisfy the unanswered questions in my soul. My own sense of failure overwhelmed me because I was sure I could have done something to prevent that terrible event. Was God punishing me? I knew then that the only one I could have called on was the Lord Jesus himself.

My life had crumbled. Would my insurance broker-husband ever work again? I couldn't even think that far yet. I could only take one moment at a time. Each day my children were my lifeline. My little Kelley would comfort me by saying things that only God could have put into her heart. I couldn't collapse or fall apart because I had to take care of my babies.

Prior to the shooting, we were like most other up-and-coming families. We were striving to be somebody as we worked through our problems. My husband was a hard worker and a good provider.

Ronald and I fought a lot, but really we weren't that much different from other couples. We had no counseling before or during our marriage to teach us to live together peacefully. Before he was shot, Ronald and I had already been going through a lot of marital problems. Fighting had become a constant part of our lives even though we loved each other. Some days the arguing got so bad, I wondered if we really did love each other. On the other hand, maybe the relationship was more than either of us could afford. God was important to us, but I didn't know that God would help us with all we were going through.

After our lives were devastated on June 16, 1974, I didn't know if I wanted to live with Ronald anymore. I kept thinking I couldn't go back to that lifestyle. I was tired and humiliated.

"You broke up our families," I told him. I didn't have real spiritual understanding, so Ronald was the only one for me to blame. After weeks of finding no peace, I turned to God—I didn't have any other place to go. God gave me strength, and I knew I had to stay with my husband. He needed me. I didn't want to stay, but I did only because God spoke to me. Even after that, many times I wanted to run away, but God wouldn't let me.

I had to learn through failure how to serve the man who had devastated my life and caused so much grief to my heart. I still blamed Ronald for everything wrong in my life, and then the Lord made me serve this man.

When he first got out of the hospital, in some ways he was nice. But soon he would say to me every day, "I'm going to kill your family one by one, and I'm going to drive you crazy."

Nothing I did pleased him. He became worse than ever. The saga continued, and there seemed no end to the abuse. No, my husband didn't change just because he took three bullets. He was still high-strung with a mean streak and a quick temper. He yelled as much as ever. When our relationship was good, it was very good, but when it was bad, it was very bad. We had, however, more good days than bad ones.

As a result of Ronald's disability, we experienced a role reversal. He stayed home with Douglas all day while I worked in the corporate world. I hated to go home at night simply because I didn't want to go into that atmosphere of anger and fighting. I used to look at the clock at work and say, "It's four o'clock and time to go home, but I don't want to go."

I longed to see my kids, of course, but the atmosphere was so bad I didn't want to be around him. From day to day his mood changed. Sometimes he was quiet; other times the fussing started when I walked inside the house. I knew he was depressed and was dwelling on his failures which made him feel even worse. Even though I tried to understand his feelings, I just couldn't keep on taking his abusive attitude. I too was angry. He had ruined my life with no visible possibility of it getting better. Now I was stuck with him, and God wouldn't let me leave him. I did the necessary things to take care of him. My marriage had become a duty, another job piled on me every day, and I seemed always tired. I made sure that he was clean and that his food was cooked. *I wouldn't let even a dog suffer*, I thought.

One day Ronald started to yell at me. We fussed for hours. When we went to bed we were still arguing with each other. In his anger he broke a thick vase over his own head. I was so frightened I ran outside and stood in the dark behind the house, praying that God would help me. I got enough strength from God that night to go back into the house.

Exasperated and fed up, I yelled, "You've tried everything, Ronald; you need to try God." That time he didn't answer. I said something about maybe he should read the Twenty-third Psalm to get an understanding of the God that provides every need. As children, we had always been taught to go to church and pray and live right before God. I had begun to pray, but I still didn't know many scriptures. Those words just popped out of my mouth.

Ronald didn't say another word. I turned over and went to sleep.

About three o'clock that morning, he woke me up and said, "Tell me about this God."

"What? I'm tired. I need my sleep, and you want to talk?"

"You're so spiritual, and you can rest so well. I can't sleep. Tell me about this Twenty-third Psalm." I sat up and talked to him about the Twenty-third Psalm by the inspiration of the Holy Spirit. I quoted the entire chapter and explained each verse as I went along.

In bed beside me, Ronald stared into space, but he didn't say anything. When I finished the last verse, I turned over. He lay quietly and didn't ask any more questions. As I went back to sleep, I felt as if the peace of God had come into the room. The next three days were the most peaceful we had ever experienced in our married life.

A few days later, he was reading the Bible. I didn't know what to say. I was so shocked to see a Bible in his hands. He looked up at me and asked, "Co, why didn't you tell me all these things were in the Bible? I've been reading all day."

I stared at him in disbelief. The change was so dramatic, I couldn't believe what I was hearing and seeing. I sat down next to him, and we talked about the Bible and God for a long time. We didn't have any cross words. I kept wondering how long this would last, but I didn't say anything. I was just thankful for the temporary peace.

Day after day he found truths in the Bible and could hardly wait for me to get home, so he could share them with me. He was smiling and happy for the first time in a long while.

I wanted to believe Ronald had changed, but I remained skeptical. We had been married nearly seven years. It was going to take more than a few days of Bible reading to wipe out all of those bad experiences. I said, "Lord, if this man has changed, you're going to have to come down from heaven and tell me, because I've been through a lot in these seven years with him. If he's changed, you've got to show me because nobody else can."

I came home from work one day and Ronald said, "Co, something awesome happened to me. I was sitting in my wheelchair and I said, 'God, I really don't know if you're real. You look real in this book I've been reading. If you're real, I want you to forgive me.' It was as if the whole world lifted off my shoulders."

Ronald didn't have any instructions from any human being concerning salvation. It came only from his reading. He was led to God by inspiration of the Holy Spirit.

I knew then that he had changed. That's when I began to love my husband all over again. This time it was in a deeper, more committed way. All the passion that we sensed when we first met came alive in us again. The old man was dead, and the new man was alive to God.

Ronald kept studying and growing. Our house became so peaceful. I wanted to believe it would always be that way. A part of me, however, kept thinking, *You'd better watch it. This is just the quiet before the storm. The hurricane is going to strike.*

The storm never happened!

He began to study the Bible with Deacon Stokes, and they grew in the Lord together. He was like a sponge soaking up the Word of God with unquenchable thirst.

God sent Bishop Calvin Williams from Cleveland, Ohio to minister in our area. Deacon Stokes brought the Bishop to our home right before Christmas of 1974.

"You've done something right," the Bishop said. Then he clearly explained salvation to Ronald and officially led him to the Lord.

He told Ronald and me to go on a three-day fast and seek God's will for us. It was the first time either of us had totally fasted for that length of time. God continued to minister to us and heal us through most of 1975. It was the best that our lives had ever been together. Ronald was so serious about the Word of God that he vowed not to leave the back part of the house from 1976-1978. God used that time to reveal the vision that is now Green Pastures Christian Ministries, Inc. No, his walk was not a physical manifestation, but he certainly walked tall in the spirit.

In 1976, we felt God wanted us to start a Bible study in our home. We invited friends to come in and learn the things we had discovered in our searching the Bible. We never intended to start a church; we just wanted to serve God.

God began to speak to Ronald and show him what lay ahead for us. We continued the home Bible study from 1976 to 1979, and then we officially incorporated as Green Pastures Christian Ministries, Inc., based on the Twenty-third Psalm. From the beginning, the Twenty-third Psalm was the foundation for our new life in Christ; therefore, it meant something special to us. Our entire ministry is centered on this revelation.

We continued to seek God, and he expanded the vision for Green Pastures Christian Ministries, Inc. As more light came to Ronald, he wrote it down. It was amazing that God showed him details about what was going to happen and what our ministry would look like. My husband saw the building and wrote down the street names as well as every minute detail of the vision. To this day, I follow the things that were written, and they are continuing to come to pass.

Our church membership increased rapidly, yet we maintained a family atmosphere. The people had known me from the beginning, and I was never a behind-the-scenes pastor's wife. My husband would always say, "If anything happens to me, ask Co. Co is here."

Looking back, I realize that Ronald was beginning to prepare me to assume leadership of Green Pastures. I didn't know what he was doing, and I don't know if he knew, but when people faced situations that needed attention, he'd say, "Co, you can handle that."

He made me responsible for ministry in every possible way. I think that was a powerful thing for a man to release his wife to be a minister. One day, the Lord told him that I needed to be ordained, and he confirmed my calling as a minister.

During those years, Ronald was in and out of the intensive care unit of the hospital as he constantly overcame complications due to paralysis and, eventually, renal (kidney) failure. The doctors often took me into the hallway of the hospital and told me that Ronald may not make it through the night. On many occasions they said he wouldn't leave the hospital alive. I would visit him and pray and read Scripture to his comatose body. Within a few days he would ask for popcorn and a television in Intensive Care, so he could watch the football game. He always came home.

The hospital stay in January of 1986, however, was different. Both of us knew it. Until then, I had always been able to go there and pray him through. But on Saturday, January 18, for the first time in twelve years, I felt a distance between Ronald and me, as if God were preparing to separate us. No matter how hard I prayed, I sensed isolation from the man I loved to hear preach, the love of my life, my soul mate. When I visited him that day, our conversation was limited. As if he had an appointment, he kept asking, "Co, what time is it?" I sat in the chair away from the bed, which was not my usual position.

Early Sunday morning, January 19, 1986, I was preparing my message for church when the Lord spoke clearly saying to kneel at the foot of my bed before I left for the service. Obediently I prayed and waited, and soon it felt like a heavy cloak was being placed on my shoulders. I was so enraptured by the Spirit of God, I didn't want to get up and go to church. I went, though, because I knew God wanted me to preach. I delivered an anointed word from God that was so powerful it shocked me. Previously, I had been active, but my role was to encourage my husband and to help him do whatever he needed to do as a minister of the gospel.

After the service, I took our secretary to dinner to honor her birthday. Then with my two children, I proceeded to the hospital.

When I arrived, I didn't feel I should take them into intensive care. The nurses were always nice to us because Ronald was a regular in-and-out patient in ICU. They always allowed our children to see their dad. However, this time I left the children in the waiting room, and I went across the hall to see Ronald.

The nurse met me as I was coming in and said, "I am sorry, Mrs. Gunby, Ronald has expired." Those words penetrated my heart like a dagger.

"Expired?" I repeated. It rang in my soul. *Expired.* He was gone. Ronald was such a punctual man. Now I understood why he wanted to know the time during my visit the day before. He had asked every five minutes, "What time is it?" He died at exactly 5:00 p.m.

The following Tuesday morning, I wasn't yet fully awake when I heard Ronald's voice, "Let me go, Co."

In my dream I heard myself say to him, "If that's what you want, I'll let you go. I'll release you."

It was my spirit talking because my flesh wanted him home and alive. I felt as if half my heart had been taken away. I felt air going through where half of my heart had been, but I released him. I was reminded that love is stronger than death, and my love for him was still holding him here. I knew I had to let him go. This time there would be no resurrections from the dead; he was not going to come back to me. I would never see those beautiful brown eyes on earth again. I knew at that point that he belonged to heaven. Although my love had brought him back to life so many times before, I couldn't do it this time. My love could not compare to the presence of God, who is Love: the one Ronald had served even unto death, the one who loves us in spite of ourselves. I said good-bye to my beautiful brown-eyed baby, the love of my life, the reason for my existence.

Since then, I've realized that out of failure came the most beautiful love relationship, love for each other and love for our Lord. Even today, I love him, and my love for him has not decreased. But I still carry on just as one who is obedient to do what God has called her to do.

My husband left a legacy for our personal family as well as our church family. When he died, Green Pastures did not own any property. We held services in rented spaces in various hotels and an office complex. I've always felt it was a Moses-and-Joshua story. God gave him the vision; I must fulfill it—I must conquer the Promised Land.

The Lord allowed my husband to come to our present location to look it over just months before his death. He went over this entire property, and he said, "I believe this is where the Lord wants us to be." We were supposed to meet for financing on Monday, January 27, 1986, but Ronald died on January 19, 1986.

After the Homegoing Celebration, I went ahead and met with the Finance Officer, Lockland Downs. It was really hard, but I had released Ronald, and I knew I was following what he wanted me to do.

At the hospital over Ronald's body, I had said, "God, if you want me to complete the work my husband began, I'm going to need triple his anointing."

In 1985, we had between six and seven hundred members. Within a year after Ronald's death, we had grown to more than fifteen hundred. In 1997, we had over three thousand in our two morning services. We had more than tripled in size!

We moved into our new building and acquired forty-two acres of land with an eight-acre lake on it. Within the next two years we purchased five properties adjacent to the church. We completed a million-dollar renovation of the church and built a gymnasium.

I heard a minister say recently, "God has programmed failure into life so that we may realize that human effort is futile without him. Our lives are testimonies of what can happen as a result of failure of manmade dreams and fantasies."

I don't think people truly know God until they reach a point of failure. We need distress, humiliation, and problems so God can birth spiritual gifts in us. God uses failure to build character, integrity, stamina, and strength. I believe through our failures we find God, and then we're able to go to the next place in him. When we look at ourselves and then look back at whence we've come, we know that it's nothing that we have done. Failure gives us a new view of God and a better sense of the reality of our limitations as human beings.

If I had not lived what you read about me today, I would never have been the woman of God I am now. I don't have a problem picking up my assigned cross, denying myself, and following him, for I know that all things work together for my good.

Kelley, Douglas, and I work full-time in the ministry. I thank God for bringing us all through the most devastating time in our lives. God truly walked us through the valley of the shadow of death, and we fear no evil because he is with us. We live and serve him with all of our hearts.

Rev. Woodrow Walker II
Senior Pastor, Abundant Life Church,
Lithonia, Georgia

CHAPTER 6

Learning from Failures

BY REV. WOODROW WALKER II

Iknew God had called me to preach when I was eleven years old, but I didn't have any idea what that meant. No one told me how to act or what to do. To make it worse, it seemed as if I got criticized for everything I did, for instance, if I listened to the wrong music or if I went to dances.

For a while I quit listening to my transistor radio and avoided Saturday night dances. I stopped whatever people criticized me for doing. Other than those things not to do, I didn't know how a preacher was supposed to act outside of church. I knew only that God wanted me to preach.

People expected me to act like a grown-up, mature preacher, or at least that's how it came across. Because of that, I felt as if I had been cheated out of my childhood. So by the time I reached my early teen years, I rebelled and began to do everything I had been criticized for.

I stayed in church, but I led two lives. One life was still donning the robe and standing before the congregation as a youth preacher. The second Sunday of every month, I preached. But the rest of the month, I was involved in fighting and running around with the wrong kind of girls—anything that other boys my age did. I grew up living in that tension—torn between ministry and being what the world considered normal.

When I was nineteen, I moved into my own apartment so I could have my freedom. That sudden freedom was a shock, and I didn't know how to deal with it. For a while, I stayed up all night just to say I had stayed up all night. Then I really went wild and tried other things, such as drinking and experimenting with marijuana.

That's how I lived, even though I continued to preach. Until 1977, when I was 27, I went to church and lived the other life as well.

That year, my life changed. By then, I had done so well with an insurance company they seriously considered me for a position as manager of one of the agencies. Big doors were opening, and I walked along the high road to success. Then I figured I didn't need the church, so I stopped going.

As a mark of my success, I received an invitation to go to Houston to speak to the Million-Dollar Roundtable. While I was there, I decided that I'd visit a church. Even today, I can give no explanation. Maybe it was just because I was alone in a strange city. (Of course, God was at work, but I didn't know that then.)

On that Sunday morning, at a small, out-of-the-way church, I received a big surprise. The people didn't act like the Sunday crowd I knew. They actually prayed—sincerely and fervently—and poured out their hearts to God. I had never seen anything like that before.

Dazed, I left the church and walked over to a sidewalk café where I ordered a Heineken. As I sipped my beer, I kept thinking, *There is more to God than I've ever experienced. God's bigger than I had imagined.*

On the plane back to St. Louis, God began to deal with me about what I had seen and heard. I kept thinking of the verse, "The earth is the Lord's and the fullness thereof; the world, and they that dwell therein" (Psalm 24:1 kjv). Even with my double life, I had memorized a lot of Scriptures.

From that time on, I began to see God in new ways. To my surprise, after returning to St. Louis, that feeling of awe didn't leave me. God intruded on my thoughts constantly.

I had planned to start taking tennis lessons the following Sunday, but I couldn't go. I kept hearing God whisper, "Go to church." Not literal words, but the feeling—the inward witness—was so powerful that I couldn't push it away.

I wrestled with that voice for a couple of hours before I said, "OK, God." I had been drinking the night before and felt embarrassed about going to church with a partial hangover, but I went anyway.

I ended up at an Apostolic Church, which is a holiness church, much like the church I had visited in Houston. Once I went inside, I knew it was exactly the right place for me. The preacher spoke about my feelings as if he knew my actual emotions and could read my heart. He spoke about emptiness—something of which I hadn't been aware until then.

My goal had been to become a millionaire before age thirty. I thought I was just driven to be successful and to live out the American dream.

Sitting in church that morning, I realized that fear of poverty and a lack of self-esteem were what kept pushing me to succeed. If I succeeded, I was sure I would believe in myself. I kept running away from childhood voices that whispered, "You'll never be anything."

I had spent years yelling back, "I'll prove myself by becoming a millionaire. I'll prove to everyone that I'm somebody."

As I listened in church that day, making a million dollars no longer seemed very important. I realized that when I went to churches in St. Louis, I hadn't gone for the spiritual blessings. Most of the time, I stared at the women in the choir. After the services, I used my sales techniques on them—and most of the time they worked.

Now things had changed suddenly and drastically. I began to cry, and I couldn't stop the tears. I hadn't cried at my dad's funeral—that whole macho thing—but this was different. The tears came, and I couldn't stop myself. I tried to hide it because I didn't want anyone to see.

Just then, the preacher said, "Young man, young woman, old man, old woman, whoever it may be, do you want to receive Jesus?"

As I stared back at him, I thought, I'm a candidate for pastor of one of the largest Baptist churches in St. Louis. Yet I'm sitting in a holiness church, and I can't stop crying. I felt I needed to respond—to go forward. I felt convicted, but I didn't go up.

He repeated his invitation, but I refused to move.

I left the church, but I did go back. When I returned—and God wouldn't let me stay away—I surrendered everything to God. He poured out his Holy Spirit on me in what Charles Finney called "liquid love" and it filled up all the empty area where the pain had been. God healed all the feelings of rejection and lack of self-esteem.

Until that experience, I had been reserved and calculating, and suddenly I found myself laughing and crying at the same time. For me, that meant being totally out of emotional control.

After that experience, I didn't care if I ever sold insurance to another person or if I ever preached again. Right then, I only wanted to please God.

Everywhere I went, I talked about Jesus, no matter whom I came in contact with. When I had the opportunity to preach, I didn't have any better sense than to share my testimony.

"There were times I came into your church," I said, "I had been at a party the night before. I was living in sin, and then I preached to you about living right."

They didn't like that. As a result of my strange behavior, my former church rejected me. Some of them called me a false preacher, but I didn't care—I was following Jesus.

I had experienced salvation in Jesus Christ, and I laid it all out to anyone who listened. Sometimes people would weep, but the pastors became angry. The doors began to close, and no one invited me to preach.

My work suffered because I no longer had a desire to sell insurance. I talked to plenty of people and would get them to the point where I was ready to close on the sale. Then, without thinking of what I was doing, I'd say, "You know, I'm not here just to sell you. There's something I want to share with you, something that happened to me."

Then I would tell them my story. Often God convicted the people. Many times they received Christ on the spot.

Obviously, my sales went down. Until Jesus Christ came into my life, I had been the number one salesman—the top African American sales agent in the company. I had won all the awards and accolades. Then I became sales agent number three. Then number four.

Within months, I became the salesman with the worst record in the company. I just didn't want to do anything but talk about Jesus Christ. My manager never lost faith in me and kept reassuring me that I was in a slump and that I would bounce back. I knew differently.

Finally, I went to the general manager and said, "I'm an embarrassment to your company because it's so much in my heart to share the gospel that I'm not doing you any good. I'm not doing me any good. I just need to share the gospel. I'll leave."

He didn't want me to leave, but I did. It was the right thing to do.

I hit bottom: no money and an empty refrigerator. I got down to bread and water and felt too embarrassed to ask my family for help. One of my cars was repossessed, and the other didn't run. I received an eviction notice. Finally, I went back to work selling insurance. Shortly after that, I asked for a transfer to Atlanta.

Within weeks of my moving to Atlanta, everything seemed to go wrong for me, and the job disappointed me. Before long, I fell out of fellowship with God and was convinced I was going to hell. Once again, I lived a sinful life.

One Sunday afternoon, I saw a beautiful woman at the mall. I introduced myself to Francine; we talked, and she told me she was engaged to a professional football player. Immediately, I thought, *She can introduce me to him, and I can use him to get me to other players so I can sell insurance to the NFL.*

Francine started to walk away, and I knew I couldn't let her. "Say, do you know any good churches in Atlanta?" I asked. "I'm bored, and I can't find a good church."

I hadn't planned to say that, but church was still in me, even more than I knew.

Francine turned around, and her face lit up. "I'm so glad you asked that." She began to tell me about the Baptist church where she went. I wrote down the name and address.

As I walked away, I knew I would see her again. I knew something else too: I was going to marry Francine.

The next Sunday I went to her church. That was the beginning of my return to God. After I had known Francine a short time, I told her about my backsliding, and she didn't turn away. With her help, along with her pastor and other ministers, I got on track with God once again. Before long, we joined a holiness church.

Four months after we met, Francine and I were married.

I still didn't care about preaching; I was thankful that I had been restored and was going to heaven, and that seemed all that mattered.

Now and then I had opportunities at church to share my testimony. They kept asking me to preach. Finally I did.

A short time later, I joined another young man, and we started a church. I didn't stay there long because I was still trying to sell insurance. But I didn't sell much. I'd set up appointments, and I'd forget sales and tell them about Jesus.

Before long, I had brought a number of people to Jesus Christ who were Spirit-filled and on fire for God. I'd take them to church, but they didn't fit in. I didn't either. In fact, I felt rejected, and it hurt because I thought I was doing something to build up the kingdom of God.

Then God spoke to me and said, "You are to pastor them, because you are their pastor."

That was really the beginnings of our church—the people with whom we shared our testimony. At first we met in our apartment, then we met in their homes. The attendance grew, so we moved to a local restaurant, and then we went wherever we could find space. For a short time, we met at the Martin Luther King Day Care Center. Our first permanent building was in Conley, on Atlanta's south side; we called the church Exciting Life. Then we outgrew that and moved around for a while. Eventually we ended up in our present building.

My life as a pastor hasn't always been a success story. I've failed many times. For instance, when our son, Woodrow III was less than a year old, my wife left the car running with the garage door open and ran back into the house for something. Woody crawled out of the car and into the street, which curves in front of our house. An 18-wheeler just missed him. A pickup truck started to make a turn and, just in time, the driver saw him and stopped. He picked up our son and brought him to the door.

I was inside preparing for my Sunday message. When I realized what had happened, I blew up. I screamed at Francine. Soon we were both crying. Finally, I called Dad Mason, my father in the ministry. "I'm not in a position to stand before my people. I'm getting ready to preach, and I have no message. That scare took everything out of me."

"The enemy could have done it whether your wife was careless or not," he said. "I'm not excusing her carelessness, but that could have happened. What you just experienced is your message. Be honest and tell them."

Sunday morning I stood before my congregation and said, "Before I preach, I have to tell you that my wife isn't with me. She's at home, and she's hurting. I am partially to blame for that." I told them the whole story and that I had repented for the way I had behaved, that I apologized to her. Then I apologized to them for failing and losing my temper.

———

I think of a time when I may have made a serious mistake. Years ago, I had the opportunity to preach for several days in California. My associate saw himself as having equal authority with me in leading the congregation. By the time I returned, all my deacons and several other leaders had rebelled against me and were ready to split the church.

When I met with them, without discussion, I said, "As of today, we have no one holding a position of leadership within this church other than me. I am now the sole leader. Those who disagree can leave. My decision is final."

Several left, but most of them stayed. Despite the loss, our church recovered. I think I handled it badly. Had I been more mature, I would have been more negotiable, and I would have reasoned with the staff.

During my early years as a pastor, I was quick on the trigger. If I saw something happening that I didn't like or agree with, I would squash it before it had a chance to become a big fire. As I've matured, I've learned to use diplomacy and not to be so quick to take action.

———

The last failure I want to share actually happened when I first went into the ministry as an adult. Those who were able to captivate the attention of an audience impressed me. I had taken courses at the Dale Carnegie Institute and had been personally trained by ministers in the area of oratory. I wanted to preach in the traditional holiness style, with the volume and charisma I observed in the top leaders.

For a while, I was the substitute preacher for an evangelist. One time he wasn't able to preach in a small Alabama town, and I thought that would be the perfect place and time to try out my lungs and start off in high gear. I was prepared to use the jargon of the evangelist, or, as some call it, to tear up the church.

That attitude reflected a character flaw within me. I didn't realize how insecure I really was in my calling and my mission before Almighty God. I could mimic others' styles and preach their messages. I was afraid of what would come out of me if I spoke by adding my own style. So I added artificial enthusiasm. I realize now, of course, that the little boy in me always wanted to be accepted.

Imitating others was the highest form of respect to me. As a child I didn't want to be just *like* my daddy—I wanted to be him. I didn't want to be *like* Roy Rogers or Wild Bill Hickok—I wanted to be them. That didn't change after I entered the ministry. I wanted to be the most dynamic, the most colorful, and the wittiest minister that I knew. To do that, I had to be those talented, high-powered preachers.

As I was soon to learn, God has a way of stripping us of our personal ambition. And my turn came.

I went to speak at the church in Alabama, and I started off in high gear, trying my best to work that small crowd that had gathered to hear from the renowned preacher and who had to settle for an unknown. I spoke in a voice about an octave higher than I normally did.

Then, right in the middle of my powerful, dynamic message, my voice left me. I couldn't speak. Not a sound. I felt totally embarrassed. Several times, I tried to speak but nothing came out. I looked around hopelessly at their faces. No one knew what to do, and I couldn't speak, so I sat down.

As I dropped my head and closed my eyes, I heard the gentle prodding of the Holy Spirit. "Now that I have shown you what not to do, you are closer to knowing what I would have you to do."

I began to smile. I knew then that God was going to bring me into a realm far beyond anything that I had ever seen or dreamed of. In that moment, God taught me that it is all right to be myself. In fact, that it is the only honest way to be. Even if I bore them, at least it would be me and not an imitation of someone else.

Right then, God enabled me to shed my desire to perform. He taught me what it means to just be. Since then, I've ignored the pull from my past to imitate the successful, to use manipulating words or tactics. I don't despise them, and I'm not jealous of their successes. I want to be faithful to whatever God desires to do in me and through me.

He's still teaching me. I always want to be a good learner.

Dr. Cynthia L. Hale
Senior Pastor, Ray of Hope Christian Church,
Decatur, Georgia

CHAPTER 7

Failure to Protect My Heart

BY DR. CYNTHIA L. HALE

My biggest failure is what I call an inability to protect my heart.

I'm relational and open to people. When I first started the Ray of Hope Church in 1986 with four people in a Bible study, that quality worked to my benefit. When we grew to forty, I could still reach out and be part of their lives. As we continued to grow, I knew I couldn't keep on.

I committed myself to reach out to the new people and assumed the original members would understand why I could no longer do some of the things with them I had done before. They didn't. At least some of them didn't. Some felt cut off from me, as if I had dropped them.

It took a long time for me to realize that I couldn't meet everyone's expectations and that I couldn't be a close friend to everyone.

Not trying to be everything to everyone has been an ongoing challenge for me. I'm learning to be intentional about setting boundaries and communicating those boundaries even when they feel uncomfortable to me. Then comes the hardest part—abiding by those boundaries myself.

That struggle affects every part of my life and ministry. Here are three examples.

The first is staffing. Over the years people have eagerly become part of the staff of Ray of Hope. Too late I learned that to some a relationship with me was more important to them than working at the Ray was. Because I didn't set clear boundaries with them in the beginning, it worked against me later.

When I had to correct them, they personalized everything. They didn't respond to me as Dr. Hale, the senior pastor, but as Cynthia who hurt their feelings. Just that fact brought conflict and pain. Part of that, of course, is their problem. But I should have been clear about the nature of our relationship.

I'm learning to say, "The work you are taking on is professional, and our relationship is professional. I like you, but I'm hiring you to do a professional job. I am not inviting you to be my friend." Those words may sound cold and harsh, but I've had to say them on a few occasions.

The second is church membership. Some members have become angry with me over the very same issue. One person accused me of false advertising. "You come across as so friendly, but you're not willing to be my friend. Who do you think you are?"

She wanted a level of friendship I couldn't give her. Women in particular say to me, "You're always talking about sisterhood. If you believe in being a sister, why won't you be my friend?"

Several women have felt rejected when I've said, "Don't call me at midnight or 3:00 in the morning." They don't understand that I have to say that to protect my heart. Even though they know we have more than sixteen hundred members, somehow they see themselves as special and deserving of all my time and attention.

Most often I've faced this when new people come to Ray of Hope, and I haven't set the boundaries clearly. They like me and ask, "Can you come over for dinner?"

When we had fifty members I didn't pause for a second thought. I'd just set a date. Now that more than thirty times that number come on Sunday, I can't say yes even though many times I'd love to spend an evening with a family.

Going to dinner signals that a personal relationship exists between us, and I don't want to convey that impression. I don't want to give a lot of attention to a dozen people and no attention to the others. I've had to accept the reality that there is no way I can develop a personal relationship with sixteen hundred people.

Third, there are my own needs. The struggle involves more than not being able to meet others' needs. It means I can't meet my needs if I continue to give myself away and use all my energy for others. At various times I've become so involved that I didn't have time for prayer, for study, or for down time and relaxation. If I don't save some time for myself, I'm not going to be effective in ministry.

For instance, during one week in early 1998 I preached three Sunday services and taught two Wednesday Bible studies, a pastors' class on Thursday, and a Saturday morning doctrinal class.

I looked at my schedule and thought, *it's almost impossible for me to prepare for all this.* I should have stopped and taken time to think through what I can do effectively in one week and said no to the rest. I didn't follow my own common sense.

Sunday and Wednesday are givens. Months earlier I had committed to doing the pastors' class on Thursday. So I knew I had those things to do. The class on doctrines, however, I didn't have to accept.

Here's where I made the mistake. One of my associates said, "Pastor, we need a class on doctrine. And you're the person who would know the most about it."

True, I was the logical one. However we have several members who are excellent teachers, and one of them could have taught the class. But I took on the class without thinking this out. I didn't protect my heart.

That's where I struggle, and that's where I sometimes fail. I have responded to needs as if I'm the only one who can meet them. Now I'm working toward a mindset that makes me pause to consider options and aftereffects.

There are some things I can't do, even though I want to very much. When I try to do everything, that's when I fail.

God calls me to do certain things, and I want to be faithful in doing them. I'm still learning that God doesn't tell me I have to do everything. I can't be everybody's close friend. I can only do what God wants when I guard my heart.

Rev. Roger W. Brumbalow
Senior Pastor, The Assembly of God Tabernacle,
Decatur, Georgia

CHAPTER 8

Presuming to Know

BY REV. ROGER W. BRUMBALOW

Before I came to Atlanta, while pastoring another church, the Lord was blessing. There was a spirit of revival in the church, and it seemed we were experiencing one victory after another. As I was looking around the church I realized that several deaf and hearing-impaired people had begun to attend. So I decided to start a deaf ministry in the church. All the ingredients were right. We had a certified interpreter, a few deaf people worshiping with us, and a large population of deaf people in the area.

Although I prayed for God's blessings on the new ministry, I must confess that I never sought God's permission or direction concerning this. After all, the need and the way to meet that need seemed sure.

When I spoke with the interpreter, in my excitement, I never asked how she felt about such a ministry. I was simply overflowing with plans of seeing a new group of people reached with the gospel.

"Here's what *I* want to do," I said. "First we'll buy a TDD; we'll get everything set up here at the church, and before you know it things will really be flowing."

My zeal was right. The need was there. What I didn't consider is that just because she was capable did not mean she was called. It didn't even occur to me—only much later did I realize—that God looks for availability not ability.

I chose her because she was capable. The fact is I drafted her! Despite my enthusiasm, I never once asked her, "Do you think God has called you to serve in this area?"

I know why she agreed to do it. I was the pastor, and she trusted my judgment.

What a mistake I had made. She was a first-class interpreter, but she really struggled with communication and people skills. She was capable—as long as she was interpreting.

After a four-week period, our deaf ministry that had begun with such momentum began to fall apart. Some of our deaf and hearing impaired people began to bring their own interpreter and refused to communicate with the church interpreter. I wondered why there was a problem. After all, this was a legitimate need, wasn't it? I had often heard that if there was a need we were to fill it, right?

Then I began to ask questions, the kind of questions I should have asked the Lord before I started the ministry. I soon discovered that my interpreter had a lot of personal and emotional problems that had begun to affect the relationship she had with both her husband and her children.

This ministry that had started out with so much promise had actually become nothing. And it was due to my poor judgment, my presumption. I had just sent her off on a mission of my own making. That ministry failed because I failed. I failed to seek God's guidance. I presumed to know more than I knew—a painful lesson—but I pray that I have learned it!

I have asked the Lord to forgive me. I mean really forgive me. There were deaf and hearing-impaired people who deserved to have a good church. They needed the ministry of the Word. Because of my bad judgment some are not getting it even today.

But more than that, the pressure I put on the interpreter created even more division in her home. She and her husband later separated and subsequently divorced. I don't believe that I caused her problems, but I am convinced even now that in my failure to seek God I certainly added to her problems.

All this happened because I desired to start a powerful ministry after seeing a powerful need. But like Joshua, I didn't seek the Lord. I failed. But as I said earlier, failure is not final in God's grace. I got on my face before God and prayed for help.

Only days later I learned we had another lady in our church who had learned sign language because of a family necessity. She came to me because she had observed that our deaf and hearing-impaired people were not being ministered to. She told me that she could interpret. Even more important, she told me she had been praying about it and felt God was leading her to that ministry.

I thanked God and rejoiced over her willingness. Then I knew that she was the person God had wanted all along. Not only did she have a heart for ministry but also the deaf community immediately welcomed her, and the deaf ministry began to grow and prosper again. Even though there were those who were wounded and never came back to our church, this woman remained faithful.

From that experience, I learned that success is a test that people sometimes fail. Success can be failure if we think we are responsible for the success. I was in a place in my ministry where the church was growing and people were getting saved. At that point of success I presumed on God. Like Joshua at Ai, I didn't seek the Lord. I made my own decision.

Now I'm learning to follow the words of the Apostle Paul: "…in everything by prayer and petition, with thanksgiving, present your requests to God" (Philippians in 4:6, niv).

Rev. Dale C. Bronner
Founder/Pastor, Word of Faith Family
Worship Center, East Point, Georgia

CHAPTER 9

Leaving the Comfortable

BY REV. DALE C. BRONNER

I had been Baptist born and Baptist bred and assumed that when I died I'd be Baptist dead. For me there was only one spiritual denomination, and I was part of it.

My own ministry actually began when I started to teach a Bible study in my parents' home. We started the studies as an outreach to my five brothers. We didn't want to be selfish, so we opened up the studies to our community. Before long we had seventy-five people crowded into my parents' house.

Despite the success of the Bible studies, we considered ourselves and our work as part of the Baptist church. I was faithful in conducting the Bible studies and often thought, *God, if this is what you want me to do for the rest of my life, I'm more than willing to do it.*

God blessed the teaching, and attendance increased. From there I felt God call me into the Baptist pastoral ministry. The congregation of Mt. Olive Missionary Baptist Church in Atlanta voted me in as their pastor.

I assumed God wanted me to stay there for the rest of my ministry. The blessings abounded. Within two years the church membership and the finances had quadrupled. My salary doubled without my having to ever ask for a raise. Everything was wonderful for me.

Then God spoke and told me to leave. God wanted me to start an interdenominational church.

For months I wrestled with that call. How could that be God's voice? For me to leave the familiar, the only church environment I had ever known, seemed impossible. For months I lay awake at night questioning and praying. At first I thought it must be demonic. Many times when I awakened in the middle of the night I'd go into my study and talk to God. "Show me what to do," I'd pray. It was definitely not a hasty discerning of the Lord's voice.

Finally I felt sure God was leading me. Once settled, I felt almost like Abraham who went out not knowing where he was going. I had to leave the familiar, the traditional, the life and people I had always known.

I told the church that I was resigning because the Lord had birthed something else in my heart and that I wasn't doing it out of a spirit of competition or dissatisfaction. Despite all I said, several members told me that I had missed God's guidance, especially when I said I was going to start an independent church.

They couldn't understand how long and hard I had struggled. It was hard for me to leave the denomination that had brought me to the faith and had nurtured me. For a long time even I couldn't understand how God would ask me to go to a place where the name *Baptist* was not out front. If it was hard for me; I know it was harder for some of them.

As I've thought of my own struggle with accepting that challenge, I've come to believe that one important thing keeping most people lumped into mediocrity is their failure to move out of their comfort zones. It took me a long time, but I finally moved because I believed God had something greater for me.

I resigned my church on one Sunday, and the following Sunday I started a new church. In that first service 125 joined the Word of Faith Family Worship Center.

To leave my established pastorate had been extremely difficult. It felt like the pain of the death of someone I loved dearly.

As I look back I realize the most challenging thing I ever had to overcome in ministry was allowing comfortable tradition to die in my life so that I could pass into the new form of ministry God had called me to.

I received some criticism. It hurt that people would think I had failed God when I rejoiced because I was following God. There were some who, once I began an interdenominational ministry, automatically cut their Baptist ties with me. That was understandable with some officials. But with others, it hurt deeply. I had, I thought, personal ties with several pastors I loved and admired. In their eyes I had failed to follow God. Although they didn't say it, I sensed that their attitude was, "If you leave our church, you must be going the wrong way."

In my thinking, I was not leaving them but simply including more people. I think they construed my actions as making a judgment against the Baptist church or saying there was something wrong with the Baptist church, which is not what I intended.

Being cut off from other Baptists meant not receiving invitations to speak in Baptist churches, and it left me feeling tremendously isolated. I had a deep craving for Christian fellowship. All of the fellowship that I had grown up with and depended on was gone. I had nothing to replace those relationships. I was instantly cut off. And it hurt.

If there was any sense of failure in those early days at Word of Faith Family Worship Center, that's when it came. Those I had loved and known, those I had respected deeply, had now turned away from me. For a long time I suffered from feelings of rejection. Finally I realized that there is always a certain amount of jealousy associated with success or growth.

At times I felt lonely, not having those friendships to lean on. But I learned to lean more fully on Jesus Christ. God brought me into contact with others who could rise above the name of a denomination or a group. Our church has continued to grow so that we now have about two thousand on any Sunday.

The numbers are not the most important. What counts most is that I am where God wants me to be. I left the comfortable, and now I'm living the challenge.

Dr. William E. Flippin
Senior Pastor, The Greater Piney Grove Baptist Church,
Atlanta, Georgia

CHAPTER 10

Failing with Grace

BY DR. WILLIAM E. FLIPPIN

When I first graduated from seminary and went into the ministry I felt I was going to change the world. I was overly optimistic about people and events.

My first pastorate was in a rural area. The members were perfectly content being rural. I was raised in the city and wanted to make that a city church. I wanted to make those leaders into what I thought they ought to be rather than what God wanted them to be.

Like many pastors in their first churches, I had something to prove. In my case, I wanted to prove that I could be a pastor. I went in a bit dogmatic and with what some call *a savior complex*. I wanted to save everybody and get each one moving in the right direction. I didn't have the wisdom or the patience to listen to them and find ways to equip them to do the work of the ministry.

In my arrogance, I told them, "I'm going to stay here three years, and then I'm leaving." Now I realize that's like getting married knowing I planned a divorce in three years, so how could it be successful? Like a lot of young pastors, I was ready to use a small congregation as a stepping stone for a larger one.

One Sunday as I left the pulpit I said to myself, "I have cast my pearls before swine." (See Matthew 7:6.) The people hadn't said "Amen" or responded as I thought they should have.

Such arrogance! I walked into my office, sat down at my desk, and cried, "Oh God, they've failed me. They've let me down." All of that turmoil because I felt they weren't being responsive to the gospel.

Another Sunday I preached one of my lesser sermons. I had hardly given the invitation when down the aisle came one of my favorite little fellows named Dennis, then about eight years old.

His coming forward shocked me. I knew that his grandmother had to bribe him every Sunday by saying, "If you'll come to Sunday school, I'll buy you a chicken dinner after church."

I hadn't preached my best that day, and the people had not been particularly responsive. Yet Dennis had responded!

I went through the formality and said, "We're glad to see Dennis come to the Lord." But I still didn't understand it.

Later, as I drove home, I kept wondering about it. *Why did Dennis join the church today? It wasn't my best sermon. The choir wasn't particularly moving. The people hadn't responded. How could this be?*

Just then I heard God speak to me—and his words changed my perspective on ministry. He said, "They're not coming to accept you. Don't ever forget that. Dennis accepted *Christ*."

Since those days I've learned a lot.

Whenever I meet any of those kind, accepting, rural people, I say to them, "I apologize for some of the sermons I preached to you, and I apologize for my arrogance."

They've always been gracious and forgiving.

Another failure has to do with the delay in the building of our Family Life Center at Piney Grove Baptist Church. We had the vision for a 27,000-square-foot building to house a gymnasium, child development center, bookstore, conference room, and classrooms.

Then came delays of every kind. The contractor had problems, and the county expressed concerns. People raised accountability questions.

"Did God indeed speak to you?" they asked. "We listened to you and stepped out, and now we're going to lose our church."

As their leader I felt helpless as if I were supposed to know everything and solve every problem. I'd gaze at the steel frame and concrete blocks as nothing happened for three months. Then the contractor put up sheet rock, and I began to feel hopeful, only to see another three months' delay without any more progress.

I'd walk around the building with depression dogging me. *Did I hear God? Did I lead the people to do the right thing? Or is this just some ego trip for me?*

The deacons understood and were with me. So was most of the congregation. I never had any ugly confrontations with anyone. But people talk, and I became slightly paranoid about it.

I'd look out the window and see two people standing in the parking lot pointing at the building. I was sure they were complaining about lack of results. From Interstate 20 drivers can see our building. I knew that as they drove by they'd ask one another, "What's going on with that building? Will they ever finish it?"

I withdrew from people. Regardless of what a good sermon I preached, or that we had baptized fifteen people, or that the church was full on Sunday, I could only think about the uncompleted building.

My eyes were in the wrong place.

Eventually we did complete our building and are proud of it. It was supposed to take a year to finish. It took three. Getting there had been hard, and I often felt like a failure. In the midst of all that, I realized that I had gotten my eyes on the building and off the important things. From then on I prioritized my life. I determined that getting the Family Life Center wasn't the most important thing. We could still have a church without it. Our first priority had to be preaching the gospel.

I've learned from my failures. Now I try to make the gospel always first and keep my eyes focused in the right direction.

Bishop Flynn A. Johnson
Senior Pastor, Atlanta Metropolitan Church,
Atlanta, Georgia

CHAPTER 11

A Failed Opportunity?

BY BISHOP FLYNN A. JOHNSON

I had a vision for an extended ministry that included a cross-cultural ministry.

We became an independent church, after having left the denomination and the building we were in. For the next two years, we moved from location to location. Then we found exactly the ideal place for ministry. It already had a church building. We had a good working relationship with the pastor who wanted to sell to us, and we were certainly excited about buying it. Before long, we were ready to sign the contract.

That may be where I failed. I honestly don't know.

A few days before we were to sign a contract to buy the building, an inner-city pastor, whom I'll call *Roy*, called. "Can we talk?" he asked. "I think it's important."

Roy and I met, and he told me, "I feel the Lord is moving me to submit my ministry to yours." He went on to propose that our two churches merge. Roy was part of a group of pastors that I fellowshipped with and I had known him for some time. If we merged, we would move into their building and would not buy the other church building.

As I listened, everything Roy said sounded fine. Yet something bothered me—something I couldn't explain even to myself. I didn't get any warning signals from God; I simply felt confused.

After I left the meeting with Roy, I prayed, "Lord, it looks like our church has been moving in the right direction. There are no major churches or ministries reaching that area. It seems right. Now Roy wants us to merge with him in a different area. What do I do?"

I decided to wait until God showed me what to do. I delayed on signing the contract.

By the following Sunday, I hadn't said anything to anyone about Roy's offer, not even the elders. I continued to pray, but no answer came. As I walked down the corridor of the school hall, one of the mothers stopped me.

"Oh, the Lord has been talking to me, and I need to tell you what God has said."

Before I had a chance to answer, she said, "I had a dream, and I saw a man come to you and submit his ministry to you. Then the two churches merged." She named several wonderful things that would happen. She was so excited about the dream, she couldn't hold it back. "I felt a mandate to tell you," she said.

I looked at her, and I said, "I want to thank you very much for what you've told me. I'll keep this in consideration." I didn't want to tell her anything because I still felt troubled, and I couldn't figure out why. It seemed as if God were answering me by speaking through the mother, but I still doubted.

A few days later, Roy and I met again. His offer was such a radical change from what we had wanted to do. Then I thought maybe I was so caught up in what I wanted to do that I wasn't able to hear God speak. So I brought my elders in on the situation. We had agreed that we wanted a cross-cultural ministry. All of that was fine with Roy. Our problem was the place. If we merged, we'd move to Roy's building. They had a small congregation and a large building that included an elementary school, and they were in the inner city.

That's where I had the problem. Moving into the inner city was different from what I had anticipated. I had thought we should buy somewhere along the perimeter highway around Atlanta. There we would have all the property we needed, the airport was accessible, there was no significant ministry within a five-mile radius, and most important, the location would offer us the opportunity to minister cross-culturally. It had seemed like the perfect solution.

I didn't know what to do. I wanted to sign the contract, but I couldn't forget the mother's dream and Roy's insistence that God had spoken to him.

I delayed signing the contract for the other building for two weeks. At night I couldn't sleep. I'd lie awake praying for guidance. One night, absolutely exhausted from the situation, I got on my knees and prayed for a long time. By the time I got up I felt it was all right to go ahead with Roy's offer. I spoke to our elders; we dropped the contract and went ahead with the merger.

Once we made the decision, it became an exciting time in our church's history. Not only did we cease to be vagabonds, moving from place to place, but also we sensed we had an opportunity to work together with a larger base of people and do the ministry we felt called by God to do.

In 1983, Roy's 35 members welcomed our 250. In order to do that, we first had to integrate the leadership. We spent many hours addressing leadership and staff issues and how to merge their vision with ours.

Never had there been more excitement over one event. Even though it wasn't a great facility, we saw potential by renovating.

When we merged, we already had a culturally and racially mixed congregation, and I felt my vision was coming true.

Unfortunately, that's where the great failure story begins.

After a few months, we discovered several shocking facts. Roy had been involved in some things that simply were not right. When I learned that, it put me in a sensitive position because I tried to restore him, assuming he would welcome my help and we'd have glorious victory together in Christ.

Naturally, Roy was upset over the facts I had uncovered. After more investigation, however, we learned there were other things more deeply buried. Roy left, of course, and it was a sad time for us. We lost one of our best elders over the ordeal, but we didn't have a church split, which was a miracle.

Our next step was to renovate the building. I started looking for loans. We got into a bond program—and actually sold the bonds—with a savings and loan company in Texas. That's when the big scandal and failures hit the S&Ls around the country.

We were sure it would resolve itself. Every week I told my people, "We're going to renovate and build additional facilities within the next few weeks." They were excited. We had great designs for renovating the building and were determined to make our corner of the world shine.

But we didn't. Week after week, we heard one story after another from the S&L that delayed us.

Most of the people didn't understand what was going on. Neither did I. Everything had seemed ready. We had a building waiting to be renovated, the people were excited, the funds had been raised, and the money from the bonds was in the bank. Then came the devastating blow: the federal government took over all the savings and loans in the country. They froze all bonds.

For the next two years, we faithfully made monthly payments of five thousand dollars. We had started with eighty thousand dollars of debt, and we only borrowed on what was half of our equity. I kept informing the people that our money was frozen, but that we were going to believe God to release it so that we could go forward. The Holy Spirit moved. New people came in and we grew. We needed more space, but we couldn't get the money to make changes.

On top of that frustration, we faced regular harassment from the left wing of the neighborhood, which wanted to get rid of us.

We were caught. We wanted to add on to our building and couldn't because our money was frozen. Finally, I flew to Texas and met with the officers of the S&L board and said, "This building is of no value to you if we can't finish it. We can't finish it because you have our money. You have the money. You have the power to release the money. Release to us the money we're due so we can at least go three quarters of the way." By then three years had passed and building costs had risen. "We're ready to build. At least we won't be liars to our people. At least we won't be paying you for what we don't have."

They would not release our money.

This becomes a long story, but in the end, what was then Boatman's Bank (which was in process of merging with NationsBank) foreclosed on us, and NationsBank then bought the property for a fraction of the cost. This meant that our people lost in every way. We had no building, and we didn't get our money back. The banks didn't break the laws, but they certainly did a lot of unethical things. The issue isn't settled, and I don't know when it will be.

So often I hear myself crying, "Dear God, is there any justice?"

While this has continued to go on, we relocated in another section of the city of Atlanta. We have 1,250 members who give. Our people have weathered the storms with me. All of us have grown in our trust of God's unfailing provisions.

Fifteen years later, I still don't understand what happened. I don't know if we failed God's opportunity for us. I know we've gone through a lot of pain and times of deep soul searching.

Yet in the midst of all this, our people have not lost heart. We're thankful for everything God's done for us. It will be interesting to see how God, who knows all things, gets us out of this.

Dr. Robert D. Lupton
Urban Community Developer, Family Counseling
Services/Urban Ministries, Atlanta, Georgia

CHAPTER 12

The Failure of a Vision

BY DR. ROBERT D. LUPTON

Isn't it a shame we only see each other at funerals?" asked a Summerhill resident as he stood talking with former neighbors who attended the wake of an elderly friend.

"Maybe we ought to have a neighborhood reunion and get together," someone else said. As the talk continued, an idea—a vision—germinated. A reunion, yes, but more: a renewed community.

A committee emerged, picked a day, and more than five thousand people came back to Summerhill—many of whom hadn't been there in more than twenty years. As they talked and many saw the devastation of their old community, some of them asked, "Can we do something to change this?"

That was the beginning of a vision that captivated my spirit. My biggest failure grew out of the most exciting vision I was ever involved in—the rebirth of the Summerhill community.

I'm an urban community developer. Although not ordained, I'm a commissioned lay evangelist, and I've done lay evangelistic work for the last twenty-seven years in inner city Atlanta. Our ministry, FCS Urban Ministries, had been involved for the previous ten years in the Summerhill community, working with street kids, counseling families, identifying homebound elderly people. We even built several houses using the Habitat for Humanity model.

For background, Summerhill is a neighborhood around the Atlanta Stadium that was once a thriving community of ten thousand people, with a healthy economic vitality, a business center, strong churches, and good schools. Racially, Summerhill has been mixed from its beginning. At the turn of the century, there was a Greek section, a Jewish section, and a Black section as well as an assortment of other nationalities. So historically it has been an economically diverse community and a healthy place to raise kids. But in the early 1950's people started to move out to the suburbs.

As people moved out, the fabric of the community became unraveled. Eventually it became an urban wasteland. The most vulnerable had been left behind to be preyed upon by the desperate who moved into the area.

Around 1990, after we knew the Olympics would come to Atlanta, I was heavily involved in the new life of Summerhill and helped to establish the neighborhood association. Together we devised a comprehensive plan for revitalizing the community. As our enthusiasm grew, we shared with capable people such as real estate developers, community planners, bankers, politicians, and others who caught the vision. We made sure that we were racially inclusive and attempted to do everything right and well.

It was an exciting time. The Olympics clock was ticking, adding additional incentive to the project. Officially we put together a development corporation to institute the real estate development aspect called Summerhill Neighborhood Development Corporation, and we recruited a board of top-quality people who could make those plans a reality.

We started the challenge of real estate development by buying the vacant Ramada Hotel with its 840 beds. We raised the money to buy it and turn it into student housing. A fine Christian builder, John Wieland, who is also the largest private homebuilder in Atlanta, agreed to build seventy-eight beautiful upscale townhouses. Through the work and vision of the board, we raised more than a million dollars to acquire properties on which to build.

We took on a public project in the middle of the community, an area that had been controlled by drug dealers. Two corporate partners,

Amoco and Home Depot, each put up three hundred thousand dollars to build co-op housing that the folks who lived there would eventually own.

The commitment level of our partners was high, and the ideas flowed. We were committed to do everything right, such as have a mixed-income, racially diverse subdivision of single family homes built with volunteers as well as market rate developers.

It was to be the rebirth of a community at the very time when the attention of the world would be focused on that very spot on the globe because of the Olympics. What an opportunity to demonstrate global reconciliation across racial and class lines!

Things started with high enthusiasm and a lot of good will from corporations, the community, and the local residents.

Of course, we faced problems. The biggest was time. We had to make many decisions quickly. Real estate developers and bankers knew their business and made fast, sound decisions, but many community members felt left out.

Empowerment and expediency started to collide. The problems increased. For example, we had to rename the hotel with a name that had a "marketing spin." The developers called it Carter Hall. Unintentionally, they bypassed the community in the name selection.

Other insensitivities of that nature happened, and we just didn't realize the impact on the community members until it was too late. The tension worsened. Six months before the Olympics, as we raced the clock, the vision disintegrated.

Because of a lot of bad history, the seeds of suspicion had already been there, so it was difficult to build trusting relationships. A few angry people fed that distrust, and eventually mobilized to fire the chair of the development corporation board, who was a highly respected real estate developer.

Once that happened, other business leaders pulled back. Within a short period of time what had been a wonderful partnership and a glorious vision lay in shambles. We heard, instead of trust, accusations and counteraccusations, bitterness, and ugly wrangling.

I was one of the casualties. My wife and I had sold our house and were ready to move into Summerhill, but we were blocked. The neighborhood corporation that owned the land wouldn't give its permission for the construction of our home to begin.

I felt the failure keenly. For nearly a decade Summerhill had been the most exciting vision I had ever been part of.

Foundations and corporations were no longer willing to invest their money. Building construction stopped. Those who managed Carter Hall were fired.

I felt physically depressed. For months I merely functioned— but not well. It was the deepest valley I had ever experienced in twenty-seven years of ministry.

God used a familiar Scripture to speak to me: the parable of the tares (Matthew 13:24-43). A farmer sowed good grain on good ground. It sprung up well, but during the night an enemy sowed weeds among the good grain. Soon the field was filled with ugly tares. That's what had happened in Summerhill. It had been good soil, and we had planted good seed, and everything was growing well. One morning we awakened and tares were everywhere. What should we do? Track down the rumormongers? Find the culprits and expose them? From those verses I realized I had to pull back, wait, and allow them to grow together, even if they threatened the harvest.

It's now long past the 1996 Olympics in Atlanta, and the relationships haven't healed much. More alienation exists now between the leaders of Summerhill than there was before we started. And the partnerships no longer exist. All is not lost, however. We actually built 260 houses. That means there are that many new homeowners in the community. Those new homeowners are racially and economically mixed. They are beginning to formulate a new vision for the community.

But some of the pain is still there for me. Instead of a person valued as a champion of community revitalization, I was viewed by some as a part of a racist, insensitive, power-hungry group of people who wanted to take over the vision. That's been painful for me to live with.

However, as I've grown through this failure, I've realized several practical things:

- Tares are inevitable. They didn't grow as a result of faulty farming or original bad seed. They are the work of the enemy, and wherever God's work flourishes, so will the enemy be at work.
- Tares take us by surprise, because we don't see them being sown. Much of it was done in darkness, and none of us could

have foreseen the devastating impact of rumor and innuendo.

- Tares are real. We can't spiritualize away their destructiveness or the real emotional pain they bring or the deep fracturing of relationships that results.
- Tares aren't terminal. The vision continues to grow through very different ways and with different people. Even though the relationships haven't mended yet the visionary fire hasn't died out.

Although I still hurt when I think of Summerhill, I'm also fired up about the new things I see God continuing to do to bring about new visions in the city. And I remind myself the harvest is God's work, not mine.

Rev. Mark L. Walker
Senior Pastor, Mount Paran Church of God North,
Marietta, Georgia

CHAPTER 13

Two Packages of Failure

BY REV. MARK L. WALKER

Failure comes in all different kinds of packages. Ministers put a lot of expectations on themselves, whether they're realistic or not. Often they can't evaluate themselves until they have failed at those expectations.

Immediately, I think of two failures as a minister.

First, early in my pastorate I faced a situation with a member of my staff. Several families in the church accused him of doing some unethical things. The staff member absolutely denied what they said. He was a man I liked and trusted, and I chose to listen to him, to support him, and not to listen to the accusations.

We confronted the families and said to them, "If you have hard evidence, produce it. If you don't, then cease from what you're doing."

All of the families left the church. It saddened me, but I thought I had done the right thing. A few weeks later I learned that the things they had said were true.

I had made a decision to support the staff member, which is what I think a senior pastor ought to do if he can. But at the time, I wasn't open enough to sit down, bring the parties together, and work toward reconciliation. I had turned a deaf ear to the families' concerns.

I felt terrible. I contacted each one and said, "I apologize for not taking the time to hear you." It was too late to get them back to our church. One of those families had been close to my wife, Udella, and me. The damage could not be undone. Even though I've seen them several times since and our relationship is all right, we no longer have the closeness we once had. And I regret that very much.

Even worse, the staff member had lied to me. I felt betrayed by him, and I couldn't trust him anymore. I had stood up for him, and he'd shot me down. I kept him on the staff, but our relationship had been badly damaged. We had lost something important in our relationship—trust—that we had to have to work well together.

I also want to share a second failure. I have a master's degree in counseling, and I took on that role along with my preaching. Within a short time, I had developed a strong counseling ministry. That's how a lot of people came to our church.

But I was doing too much and didn't realize it.

That overinvolvement hurt on two fronts. First, I had become so involved with people who hurt that I wasn't always available to develop leadership and set a vision for the people; I got bogged down too much in the hurts of other people. Second and more important, my counseling caused a strain on my marriage.

I became too involved with some of those I counseled, and before long they depended on me. That wasn't healthy for them and certainly not for me. I could only think that I was helping them.

Then they began to call me at home. They were already taking up a lot of my time at the office, and now they were calling at night for counseling.

"I think you're getting overinvolved," Udella said.

I didn't really hear her, and pointed out that I was serving God and helping hurting people. My wife kept insisting that I was allowing my counseling to take up too much of my time. My preaching was suffering and so was my administration of the church. But I would not listen.

Finally one night after an exhausting day of counseling I was so emotionally, psychologically, and physically drained that I could not find the energy to prepare my sermon for Sunday. I was spent. I could not hear from God. I knew then that things had to change.

I began by asking God to forgive me for not listening to him—or my wife. I also sought forgiveness from Udella. I then had to adjust my entire schedule.

I cut back on my personal counseling and began referring people elsewhere. Some of those I was seeing took offense to my new approach, but I had to do what I knew was right.

In all my counseling studies my instructors repeatedly warned the students about overinvolvement, but I knew that wouldn't ever happen to me. However, it did. And before I knew it I was there. I felt like a failure. I felt like I'd blown it.

Since then I have changed my strategy. When people come to me for counseling, I see them two or three times. If they still need help, I refer them to someone else. We have several lay counselors here and a counseling service.

I had failed. But I learned from my failures.

Rev. Byron L. Broussard
Senior Pastor, Greater Rising Star Baptist Church,
Atlanta, Georgia

CHAPTER 14

Under Siege

BY REV. BYRON L. BROUSSARD

I had been called to a relocated church that wasn't prepared for the reality of a growing ministry. Before I ever came on the scene, the congregation had split and dismissed several ministers. I'm not sure why they called me, but they did. The church wasn't growing, and it faced a lot of problems, but I accepted the call anyway.

My first failure came when I confronted a fractured and volatile remnant that had come with the relocation. I asked how much money we had. The small staff hadn't been paid in three months, and I knew we needed to do something. As their pastor, I asked for complete fiscal accountability—which I discovered quickly hadn't been their idea of the role of the pastor.

"As a church, you are broke. You don't have a sophisticated management system," I said to the finance committee. "I cannot pastor this church if I don't know where everything is. By the beginning of next week I expect you to have gathered the little scrap pieces of paper—or whatever things you keep accounts on—and get them to me so I can review them and see where we are. We owe three million dollars on our building alone. I need to know where we are if I'm going to lead you."

They worded it differently, but the effect was, "We won't do that."

The battle line was drawn, and I wasn't going to lose. After the committee left, I borrowed a hand truck and picked up the church safe. I rolled it down the hall and put it inside my secretary's office. "I want you to type a log," I told her. "No one writes a check unless they have authority for it. We're going to have a system of responsible internal controls."

The word spread about what I had done. I could survive the resistance, but I needed the congregation on my side. To avoid a polarization I began to speak openly to the Sunday morning congregation about financial accountability.

Over the next few months we lost a few people, especially the older ones who didn't want things to be different. In some ways that hurt because I wanted to be able to make everybody happy. Eventually I admitted to myself that I couldn't please everyone.

Fortunately for me, Lamar, the man who had chaired the deacon's ministry, had a vested interest in my success. He had brought me to the church and encouraged the people to vote for me. He didn't feel he could turn around and abandon me. Every day he visited the church office. At first, I think, he was watching me—waiting for me to do something to upset him enough so that he could turn against me. Before long, however, he began to understand and became truly supportive.

More than anyone else, Lamar stopped me from failing. Those who didn't like me said I was too young, that I didn't care about old people, and that I wouldn't visit the sick. He took me to visit people who were ill. He marched me through neighborhoods and into homes. He made sure people knew who I was and that I was visiting. He took me places in his car I know I wouldn't have gone on my own and probably wouldn't even have been able to find. Without Lamar I'm not sure I could have survived that critical period.

By the end of the first year our membership had grown from 150 to a net gain of 480. The second year it was over 500. Within three years we had become virtually a new church. Yet the people who had been there when I came still held the major positions of responsibility. They punished me by withholding their offerings. As the church continued to grow I set higher standards. For instance, I said, "If you do not give at least a tithe—a tenth—of your time, talent, and money, you can not participate in the decision-making process."

I faced a volatile and hostile camp that fought me every step. It saddened me that they were unable to see their hardness. By contrast, the new people coming in accepted whatever I asked of them.

Thinking about those who left, with some of them I went to the graveyard. I buried more than forty the first two years I was at the church. Others left with anger and unforgiveness in their hearts. More than one person charged that I had stolen the church from them. Those accusations hurt, especially in the beginning, but I knew that was the cost I had to pay if the church was going to grow.

For months I believed I was alone and felt I was constantly under siege. I honestly didn't think of quitting because I believed I was supposed to be there. They were a small group, although very vocal. They were losing power, and maybe that's what upset them most—they were losing their control on the church.

For four years the siege continued. At one point, that small group became so angry that they decided to expose me. While we were in worship the disgruntled—still members—put flyers on the windshields of cars in the parking lot. As I remember, it started out with these words: "This is a letter from some concerned members. We want you to know who this man is." They called me Jim Jones and David Koresh combined and charged that I was deceiving everyone. They attacked the finances of the church (ignoring how bad they had been until I took charge). They assailed every program I had started.

The morning they put flyers on windshields, Atlanta Mayor Bill Campbell worshiped with us to endorse my ministry. Publicly he said that I was a fine man and that he was looking forward to seeing the success of our ministry.

After worship I met with forty people who were joining the church. Someone brought the letter to me. I glanced at it and kept teaching the intake class. To anyone who observed me, I treated it as if it were nothing. But inside I felt crushed. I had tried so hard to do the right things. The church was growing, but that small, vocal group seemed determined to fight in every way possible. The cruel statements and outrageous lies hurt. I felt the insults as personal attacks, and they hurt.

I knew I'd made mistakes. Part of it was moving too quickly. Should I have been more tactful? If I had would things have been different? A hundred times I asked myself those kinds of questions and tried to second-guess what I might have done better.

At one point the same people even filed a civil lawsuit because of changes I had made. I felt they were ruthless. They lied, and that hurt the most.

I survived. Eventually the members of that opposing group died or left the church.

Today the church is healthy, and we're still growing. But I can never forget it wasn't always that way. It started with failure.

Rev. Brenda C. Chand
Minister, Trinity Chapel,
Rex, Georgia

CHAPTER 15

Failure Lasts a Long Time

BY REV. BRENDA C. CHAND

My earliest memory begins when I was about two years old. I woke up and couldn't find my mother. "Where is Mommy?" I asked my dad.

"She's gone." That's all I remember him saying.

We lived in a small trailer in Michigan, and snow covered the ground. I got dressed and went outside to look for her. I found her headscarf on the porch railing. She had run away in the middle of the night.

Mom came back, and only years later did I learn what had happened. Dad frequently got drunk and abused her. That time, she had run out of the trailer in such a hurry she didn't put on her shoes and dropped her scarf on the railing. She had run into the Michigan snow and spent the night in a little shed. There she found some old books and used their pages to wrap around her feet.

For most of my childhood, we lived in terrible poverty. There were five children, and at times, all seven of us lived in one room. Dad never stopped drinking, at least not for long. It became a predictable pattern. We would move, Dad would get a good job, everything would seem fine, and then he'd get fired for drinking on the job or fighting with someone.

Childhood, of course, wasn't happy. He didn't beat us the way he did Mom. For us, it was mostly verbal abuse. We begged her to leave him. "We'll do anything we have to do. Just leave him. Let's get out of this."

She wouldn't do that. She stayed with him until the day he died.

Today I look back and see the contrast in my lifestyle then and now. From seven of us living in one room to the spacious home we have today, there is a kind of success story. But there's a lot of failure in between the two places. And even some failure today.

Dad would never let my mom go to church. If she did, she had a high price to pay. He insisted she was only going there to meet a man. I heard that accusation for years. But she often went anyway, and she made sure we went with her.

In time I went forward at church to surrender to Jesus Christ. I was afraid of what Dad would say about it. Surprisingly, he gave me a hug and then said, "You're not at the age of accountability. Don't worry about this stuff too much."

That was the only hug I can remember receiving from him in my life.

After I finished high school, I moved to Atlanta to go to Beulah Heights Bible College, where I worked in the office. Sam Chand and I were in the same class, and we fell in love and married after our graduation. Sam became a pastor in Michigan near where my parents lived.

During the eighth year of Sam's ministry, things changed with my father. He had never come to his own kids' church plays or programs. But with the birth of grandchildren, he acted differently. He loved the kids and showered them with attention in ways he had never shown us.

Dad's lifestyle began to take its toll. One Sunday night he was really sick, and he knew it. He said to my mother, "I think I'm going to go to church tonight."

"Well, I think I'm going, too," Mama said.

When Dad walked into the back of the church, our eyes met. Tears filled both our eyes, and I knew—even though we had not said a word—that he was a changed person.

Something was different and it showed. He prayed and read his Bible often. Many times, he asked Sam to come over and pray with him. Yes, he was a changed man.

One Sunday afternoon, I sensed that Dad was nearing the end of his life. As Sam's wife, I had done everything in the church from teaching Sunday school to visiting the nursing home. I never missed a service. But I felt I needed to miss church that evening and go to see my father.

I had a mission, a very simple one.

I had never heard my dad say, "I love you." And I had never said, "I love you" to him. My mission that night—and I knew it had to be that night—was to tell him that I loved him. Although I didn't expect to hear him say the words to me, I hoped he would.

At the hospital we were alone in his room, but we wouldn't have much time together because Mom and my sister were on the way.

As I looked down at him, I thought, *It's now or never.* Several times I opened my mouth to speak, but the words wouldn't come out. I prayed silently, pleading with God to help me. I had to say the words to him while he was alive to hear them.

I took a deep breath and said, "Dad, do you know that I love you?"

"Well, I'd whip you if you didn't."

"But do you know that I love you?"

"Well, that's all that any of us have."

It wasn't much of an answer, but it was all he was able to give, and I knew it. I also realized then that he'd never speak the words I wanted most to hear.

As I continued to stare at him, I began to feel foolish. *He's going to get better tomorrow,* I thought, *and when he does, he'll laugh at me. This will become a big joke to him.*

Dad didn't laugh at me.

He died the next day.

Even as the tears flowed, I realized how close I had come to never telling him that I loved him. Though I'd never hear those three words from him, I had done the right thing.

In sharing this story, I realize how much my childhood has affected my whole life. It made me more concerned that my children knew they were loved. But I've missed many opportunities to express love because I didn't know how or simply couldn't do it. For many years I didn't know how to get close to other people. Maybe I didn't want to be in a position to get hurt, as I had been with my dad. Consequently, many people think I'm not only quiet but also standoffish. I want to reach out, but it's a constant battle for me.

Here are two examples. First, Sam and I were in a seminar, and a woman was there—a good friend. At the end of the meetings, she was crying. Sam said, "Just lay your hand on her and pray for her."

"No," I said. I couldn't explain. It wasn't that I didn't want to reach out to her. I just couldn't. I felt I had failed her.

Second, in 1997 I started a Bible study with women, and a neighbor attended. She said that she had been hurt by things in her church and hadn't been back. After five months, she pulled me aside and said, "I have to have prayer."

Instead of me praying for her, I called someone else to do it. I cared and I knew she was hurting, but I simply couldn't pray aloud for her. She was reaching out to me, and I could think only that I had failed her.

Unfortunately, I could tell story after story of my failure. And for me, it is failure. Yet I know God is with me and is working in me. Every time I reach out—and I'm slowly beginning to—it takes so much out of me. But I want to be open. With the Holy Spirit's help, I know I can.

Failure can last a long time, but it doesn't have to last a lifetime.

Rev. H. Allen Skelton
Founder and President, White Fields
Ministries, McDonough, Georgia

CHAPTER 16

Failure: Growing in Reverse

BY REV. H. ALLEN SKELTON

On January 1, 1983, I didn't think my life could get any better. Six months later, I could barely remember how to smile.

For nine years I had prayed for doors to open for me to go into full-time ministry. Then the elders of the church where I had faithfully worshiped and served for seven years asked me to become pastor.

When they asked me, I felt elated. At last I would be the pastor of a church! God had fulfilled my prayers and my dreams. I knew we were ready to move forward, and I could hardly wait to incorporate all the great ideas I had been studying and storing up. Once I put them into action, we would really grow.

During the first weeks, with overwhelming zeal, I started putting into practice everything I knew and had read that would guarantee a successful pastoral ministry.

I did all the important things I had heard and believed would build a powerful, growing church. After all, my ideas were first-class and proven by the experts. For instance, instead of just preaching sermons, I put together teaching series on subjects everybody cared about. We disbanded the choir and formed a praise team. All the "happening places" I had visited were distinguished by their new approach to song ministry. I loved what I saw in those places. It seemed reasonable to convert our old structure into something more attractive that would draw sinners and saints.

Surely everybody in the congregation would love my ideas, applaud my vision, and get behind me. My theory was the better equipped I was, the easier it was going to be to do something great for the Lord.

I set out to instill confidence in the existing leadership and to let everyone know we were charting a new course. Nothing could stop us. That seemed reasonable since I was sure that God had given me the opportunity to pastor in the first place.

Then I discovered something. Rigorous training wasn't enough. The problem with my vision and power-laden ideas was simple: they just didn't work. Instead of people flocking into worship services, they began to stay away.

Every week attendance shrank.

What was wrong? I asked myself. *Was it my fault? Was it our building? Our location?* I thought everything through again and again. The church facility was attractive and in a good location along an arterial highway, so that wasn't the problem. Was I the problem? So far as I knew everybody loved me. What more could a young, energetic pastor ask for?

For years I had been reading the right books on how to lead successfully, attending some of the best seminars available, studying part-time at Beulah Heights Bible College, and listening to advice from some of the most successful pastors around.

I consoled myself by reasoning that it was natural for a few to leave when a new pastor took over. There were always disgruntled people who resisted change. But after six months, more than half the congregation had gone.

Finally, I woke up. I came to the realization that my excuses for failure were just that—excuses. I admitted something else: my dreams weren't their dreams. My methods—supposedly failure-proof—just didn't work.

I was a failure. It hurt to admit that. My dream of overhauling a denominational church and converting it to an inspiring contemporary church quickly faded.

We grew—in reverse. A number of people wanted to believe in me and in my plans, but nothing I had instituted had proved to work. My improvements meant the loss of more members. Nothing stopped the loss.

I wanted to quit. The church could grow if I left, I thought. We had good leaders in the congregation. Surely, they could do more than I could. I would go back to repairing computers for a living and be an active layman. After all, I knew what to do when a computer broke, but how could I fix a broken church?

Fortunately for me, I came from a home where we hardly ever experienced quitting. My father rarely gave up on anything he felt the Lord had given him to do. He often paid a tremendous price to persevere, but to him the principle of being faithful to a cause was motivation enough to carry him to many successes.

I couldn't run away. I knew that. So I continued to pray. More than ever, I had to find out how to turn the church around.

Although nothing seemed to be going right, I remembered that even David had his Ziklag where he had to encourage himself. I sought the advice of a few godly men. They spoke and I listened. Soon I realized the main problem hadn't centered in me or in the changes, but in the procedures I had used to bring about change.

I decided to regroup.

The following Sunday, I admitted to the congregation my over-ambitiousness and asked them to persevere with me. Forgiveness and acceptance showed on their faces.

For the next three months, we continued to lose members. But those who stayed became more committed than ever. They worked with me to bring about the changes we needed to reach the people we were living among.

After another six months, the attendance stabilized. New people visited and joined the church, and our numbers slowly climbed. But more than numbers, the enthusiasm and commitment grew. As I felt their support, my confidence grew too.

I didn't realize how soon I would go through the whole cycle again.

We had problems—big ones—after we decided to relocate the church thirteen miles away. The church

- lost $70,000 to a dishonest contractor,
- fired the second contractor and made me the contractor,
- faced testy building inspectors.
- besides all the problems at the church, I had personal problems during that period of time, such as,

- tension at home fueled by my overinvolvement in ministry and underinvolvement with my family,
- the impossible task of being full-time contractor, pastor, husband, and father,
- financial problems,
- tremendous pressure trying to keep up with all there was to learn about people and pastoring.

The question for me became not whether I would fail but whether I would fail more often than I succeeded. As the struggles continued, I reminded myself of something I had heard many times in my life: The big difference between someone who does exploits for God and one who doesn't is simple. Those who fail don't get back up one more time.

Once we started our turn around we succeeded on many levels, and I'm thankful to God. I'm most aware that leadership is a journey. It's not a destination, but a conscious, continual decision to go forward regardless of obstacles.

My confidence to lead hasn't come from a flawless record. It has come from learning the many ways not to go about doing something. I had to fail before I could succeed.

Rev. Carolyn A. Driver
Founder/Spiritual Leader, Carolyn Driver
Ministries, Tyrone, Georgia
Instructor, Beulah Heights Bible College

CHAPTER 17

Listening to the Wrong Voices

BY REV. CAROLYN A. DRIVER

Tony's addiction to drugs had gotten him into trouble with the law.

"I need your help," he pleaded.

I was the associate pastor of a church, and because Tony needed my help, I eagerly did whatever I could. I talked to the arresting officer and to the judge. I contacted Teen Challenge Drug Recovery Program and filled out the papers for his admittance into their program. I set up his appointment with the doctor for his physical before he could get into Teen Challenge.

After two weeks of nonstop helping Tony, it was time for him to leave for Teen Challenge in North Carolina. Only hours before he was to leave, he changed his mind and decided he didn't want to go. His refusal affected my credibility with the arresting officer, the judge, and my Teen Challenge contacts. His behavior made it harder for me when I tried to get help for other kids.

Why did I work so hard and try to do so much for Tony? Had I asked myself, I would have said, "I love Tony. He needs my help. He and his family depend on me to do everything I can for him, even though he disappoints me." That wasn't the real reason I had helped him, but I didn't understand it then.

There was another clue. Because I could get a lot of things done, my senior pastor kept giving me more to do. Before long, I realized that I consistently worked at the church office long after everyone else had gone. Many times I returned to work at night. I didn't want to disappoint my pastor, who counted on me, and he was the authority. If I didn't perform, he might not like me or he might think I was a bad associate pastor. So I worked harder.

I had counseled a couple who constantly fought. They had already made the rounds to every pastor and counselor at the church with little or no change in their situation. When the phone rang one night, I had already worked sixty-nine hours that week. I had been in bed less than an hour.

"This is Sue. Please come over and talk to us. Bob and I are fighting again. Pray with us. We need your help."

My common sense said "No" and so did my exhausted body. But Sue knew how to push my buttons of need, emotion, and expectation.

"We really need you," she said. "You're the only one we could call." She went on to say that no one understood them like I did; no one else could touch the throne of God in prayer for them but me.

I dragged myself out of bed, dressed, and drove to their house. There I counseled and prayed with them until 7:00 that morning.

When we finished, Bob and Sue went to bed. I couldn't do that; I went home to shower and then report to the church before 9:00 a.m. for a full day's work.

———

Those examples are typical of the major mistake I'd made throughout my life and ministry. All my life I'd assumed that all good things were right things. As long as they were good things, they were God's will. Because I believed that, three voices ruled my life. They were the voices of need, emotion, and others' expectations of me.

For years, I felt responsible for the world and everyone in it. Secular psychologists have a term to describe that attitude and behavior: *codependency*. The simplest definition of codependency is "people who love too much and end up victimized."

If someone had a need that I could meet, I assumed I was supposed to do it. I didn't think to ask God if he wanted me to meet the need. Why should I? It just seemed obvious that I should do a good thing.

Sometimes I did things, said things, and went places not because of others' needs only but out of my need to be needed. Too many times (I realized later) my emotions determined my choices, especially if it was a positive emotion.

When it came to others' expectations, especially if they were authority figures, I never hesitated. It took a visitation from the Holy Spirit to deliver me from managing my life by those three voices. God used two Scriptures to help me see how I had failed, even though I was doing nothing but good things.

First, from John Chapter 11 (Lazarus' resurrection story), the Holy Spirit showed me that those same three voices spoke to Jesus. When he heard that Lazarus was dying, his emotions wanted him to go to his friend. Lazarus' life-and-death need called out to him. Mary, Martha, and the crowd at their home in Bethany expected him to come.

Those voices must have pulled heavily on Jesus that day, yet he said, "I don't go anywhere unless Father says 'Go.' I don't do anything unless Father says to do it, and I don't say anything unless Father says to say it."

In the second Scripture passage, Jesus said that one day people would come to him and list all of the things they had done in his name (Matt. 7:21–23). He would call them evildoers and declare, "I never knew you" (v. 23 niv).

How could that be? They healed the sick. They cast out demons. Preached the Word. And yet they were evil. As I read those verses, the Holy Spirit spoke to me, and I understood. They were evil because they did things God hadn't told them to do.

God showed me that not all good things are the right things. The only right things are those God tells us to do. Because I had been listening to those three voices and assuming they were God's voice, I obeyed them.

For thirteen years, I worked between fifty-eight and seventy hours a week because I allowed myself to be directed by the voice of need, the voice of emotion, and the voice of others' expectations of me.

The Holy Spirit delivered me from those voices and from codependency. But the healing didn't occur instantly. I had a complete physical breakdown that lasted for eighteen months—I suffered from deep depression and struggled with constant anxiety attacks. I would either sleep too much or couldn't sleep at all. My emotions were frazzled, and my perceptions were skewed. It had been a costly mistake to listen to those voices. After my recovery from codependency, I promised God that I would stop listening to those three voices.

As I reviewed my life, I realized that I had trained people to know that I would be available twenty-four hours a day, seven days a week. Once I started checking with God before doing anything, I soon eliminated at least 85 percent of my activities.

At first, those people were upset, naturally. But they got over it. God wants us to walk with others through troublesome things, not to become their god or take over the work of the Holy Spirit. Often we short-circuit what God is doing in the lives of others when we fix and rescue.

My role is to pray and obey God's voice.

A few months after my deliverance from listening to the three voices, I met with the senior pastor so I could go over my schedule and responsibilities with him. "I want you to help me prioritize my work load," I said.

When he saw my work load, he admitted, "I had no idea you were working all those hours with no days off just trying to do all the things I gave you."

Not long after that, I received a phone call from Sue. "Bob and I are fighting again. Oh, we need you, Carolyn. You're the only one—"

I told both of them to get on the phone. I prayed for them and told them to meet me at my office the next morning at 10:00.

They didn't like it. "We have other things planned for tomorrow," she said.

They had wanted me to make a decision based on their emotions, their needs (or my need to be needed), and their expectations of me. They didn't come to my office, and they never called me again late at night.

Two years after Tony had turned down his opportunity to go into drug rehab, he came by to see me. "I need help. This time I'm really serious," he said.

"I'm glad you're ready," I said. "Now first, you need to call the judge." I gave him the phone number. After he called Teen Challenge and received the application forms, he filled them out by himself. "I'm here to encourage you," I said.

From time to time I still hear the three voices. Instead of rushing out to obey them, I pray for Father God to direct me. My life works better that way.

Rev. Jacquelyn B. Armstrong
Instructor/Assistant to the President, Beulah Heights
Bible College, Atlanta, Georgia

CHAPTER 18

A Second Chance

BY REV. JACQUELYN B. ARMSTRONG

In 1985 when God called me into the ministry, I was so spiritually immature, I didn't know what to do or how to handle the call from God. During this time I made the mistake of turning to man for understanding rather than turning to God.

When I first understood that God was speaking to me about doing a special work in the ministry, I thought I was losing my mind. I didn't understand that God talked to people in such a way.

A Christian friend assured me that I wasn't going crazy and encouraged me to seek God for an understanding of the call. As I did that, God made it clear that he was calling me to preach his Word.

Then came the problems. I faced opposition because I was a woman and unmarried. Suddenly I began to feel shunned. That seemed strange. Until I made it known that I had a calling on my life there had been plenty of opportunities to teach, speak, and do things in the church. Once I announced the call, doors began to close. People I thought of as friends or confidants seemed to turn away from me, and I didn't understand. I couldn't speak or teach with the freedom I had before.

131

"God, what is going on?" I asked. "I thought you'd open doors, and now they seem to be closing on me."

One thing I now realize as I look back is that I didn't understand God's ways.

Also when I was just a worker in the church without a title, my ministry was accepted. After I said God was calling me to be a minister, the announcement seemed to change everything. I believe those in leadership roles began to see me differently. Because of my immaturity, I wasn't spiritually ready to cope with the situation.

Being in the church and listening to the teaching and preaching, I had a mental image of what ministry was. I started going after that kind of picture without the knowledge and understanding of what was really involved in ministry.

A good friend from whom I had expected a lot of support seemed to turn against me. And at times even treated me rudely. This attitude change in someone that I so totally depended on deeply hurt me.

I talked to a friend about it and was assured that I was not alone. My situation seemed to be the norm among women in ministry.

After that ordeal I went on with my life. I got married, and my husband, Wendell, and I started attending a neighborhood church. I quickly became involved in teaching Sunday school, teaching women, ministering in every way I could. Until then I hadn't said anything about being called.

One day I felt it was time to speak up. I told the pastor that God had called me to teach and preach.

Knowing that my husband did not have a special calling on his life, the pastor shook his head. "A woman can't go in the ministry unless her husband is in the ministry."

I had never heard such a thing. Nevertheless he was the leader. If he said it, it must be true. He talked to my husband, who definitely didn't feel called, although he supported me in my calling. Again, the pastor said he didn't believe God would call a woman if he had not called her husband.

After that meeting, my world collapsed. The doctors called it anxiety, but I knew it was depression.

That depression lasted two or three years. I had listened to those in authority, and when they closed the doors, I didn't know what to do or where to turn. I didn't want to minister anymore. I felt rejected by everyone. I couldn't cope with my job, and I couldn't cope very well at home. I did the things I was supposed to do but without any interest, just going through the motions. It was as if nothing mattered anymore.

I had a burden to teach, and God didn't stop talking to me. But the doors were closed, so how could I teach? How could I do what God wanted me to do? Or was I really crazy, and it wasn't God speaking? Yet in my heart I knew I had heard God speak.

It didn't occur to me to bypass people and go directly to God. As long as I'd been a Christian, I'd been accustomed to going to somebody else for counsel—a preacher, a teacher, or someone— whenever I had a need. Over the years I talked with others and had them pray for me.

Now I had come to a point where there was nobody for me to go to. Only later did I realize that God was trying to position me to go to him rather than people. It took a long time for me to realize that God was the only answer.

Then came the day I hit bottom. I had been invited to preach a Sunday morning service. After I had preached what I thought was a good message—and I could tell from the response of the women that they were listening intently—I proceeded to invite persons with needs to the altar for prayer.

I extended the invitation, but no one came forward. The women had responded so well to the message, and their faces and voices made me know they had heard and wanted to respond. Something was wrong, but I had no idea what it was. I gave the invitation again, but no one came. In fact, some of the women sat down. I felt embarrassed, so I stopped, turned around, and went back to my seat on the platform. Then another minister came forward and extended an invitation, and several women came forward.

Humiliated and embarrassed, I didn't know what to say or do. I didn't understand what was going on. Later, I learned that the problem was that I was not ordained and, therefore, had no authority to minister an altar call.

If that was so, why had I not been told? I thought.

After that experience, I was really confused about ministry. I walked out of there feeling worthless and totally rejected. All I could think was that something must be wrong with me.

A few days later, I began to have chest pains. Wendell took me to the hospital, and it was diagnosed as an anxiety attack. I know only that I was sick in my soul far more than in my body. I was falling into deep depression, didn't understand it, and didn't know what to do about it.

I continued to struggle. How could God give me a gift to preach, call me into the ministry, and not make a way for me to use that gift?

For years, of course, I had heard about Beulah Heights Bible College. One day I thought about taking a writing class because I liked to write. I wasn't working full-time, so I decided that while I was at home and not working, I could write. Maybe it would help to pull me out of my deep hole.

I enrolled in January 1994. From that day on, my life changed. I felt accepted. I knew I belonged there.

After a few weeks of studies, the President, Dr. Samuel Chand, called me aside. "Would you consider coming to work for me?"

I couldn't believe what I had heard. Somebody wanted me. I hadn't been good enough to minister in a church, but I was good enough to work for the college. I was good enough to help train those who were going to be pastors.

I couldn't figure out why he wanted me. I thought, *Maybe this is a trick*; but it wasn't. Dr. Chand apparently saw something in me—something other leaders had not seen—and it hadn't threatened him. I called Wendell, we talked about it, and I went to work for Beulah Heights. I've been there ever since.

God has used people at Beulah Heights to heal me. I have always felt accepted there and valued for myself and the ministry God has given me. I'm now ordained—doors are open to my ministry in the north, south, east, and west—and I have a full ministry with students at Beulah Heights.

Yes, I went through a lot of pain and suffering. But out of that pain and suffering God birthed a powerful ministry. God gave me a second chance, and through that experience I learned to put my trust in him.

Mrs. Gloria E. Spencer
Freelance Writer, Atlanta, Georgia

Failure is for Everyone

BY MRS. GLORIA E. SPENCER

Failure isn't limited to the twentieth century. The Bible relates many instances of it. In fact, virtually every person in the Bible failed in some form. I'm not just talking about the bad or the insignificants. God's champions—the specially created, chosen, and commissioned ones—failed. And their foibles are openly reported.

Adam and Eve had almost a perfect ministry; their calling in life was to make the earth beautiful and fill it with children to enjoy it. God created Eve—fresh, innocent, childlike. I think of her in terms of Liesl von Trapp from *The Sound of Music.* Her much older, wiser suitor, Rolf, referred to her as " … an empty page that men will want to write on."

Satan moved in on Eve's innocence and tempted her with the idea that she could be wise. "Just eat this, and you'll know what you're missing." And he wrote on her a message that has passed down to all of her daughters for hundreds of generations.

What about Adam? Did he realize what he was doing and do it anyway? Or was he as naïve as she? Either way he took a detour from the mission and ended up losing his commission.

Then there's Father Abraham, one of God's special ones, cho-sen to be the father of nations. But there was a problem. Abraham was childless and already past the prime of life.

Abraham has been called the father of the faithful. To his credit, he waited twenty-five years for God's promise to come true. In times when passing on a heritage to the next generation meant everything, that was a long, long wait. I imagine Abraham had days when he believed the boy would surely come that year. He probably had other days when he thought, *Sarah's past the bearing age, so how can we possibly have a child?*

When his wife suggested a solution, I can understand how the idea looked pretty good. She said, "Take my maid. Have a child by her." Neither Abraham nor Sarah, it seems, stopped to consider all the gut-wrenching consequences.

Years later one of the psalmists wrote, "Blessed (happy) is the man that walketh not in the counsel of the ungodly" (Psalm 1:1 kjv). I'm not saying that Sarah was ungodly, but her counsel cer-tainly was, and a lot of grief ensued that still exists today.

Samson, the strongest man who ever lived, comes to mind. A man chosen by God, he killed many of his enemies during his life-time. But the inability to control his wild nature led to his downfall at the hands of a woman.

In any accounting of biblical failures, King David has to come to mind. If there ever was a natural-born hero, it was the courageous warrior and sensitive, creative musician. Born to a family of herders, his light couldn't be hidden among the sheep. While still a boy, he delivered the nation from a nine-foot nemesis and years later became the divinely chosen king of Israel.

David was a man who knew God, and many of his psalms began with a complaint as he poured out grief, sadness, anger, revenge, and confusion. But before the lyrics close, he is often restored to quiet, grateful resignation to the plan of God.

How could such a man commit adultery, conspiracy, and mur-der? It baffles the mind until we realize that any of us is capable of that and perhaps more.

Isn't it comforting that God knew it all along? Before David was anointed, God knew, and none of his failures surprised God. David wasn't chosen because God couldn't find any better person. It's just that failure is part of living and learning. It's part of the making of us, like steel being tempered with fire and water. God knew all that David's heart contained even when he called him, "a man after God's own heart" (1 Samuel 13:14).

Or what about Solomon, the wisest man of all time? I wondered how a man so close to God could allow his heart to be drawn away. Then I realized that when things are going well in my own life, it's easy to neglect my time with God and to lose the intimacy with Jesus Christ. When it's happened to me, I felt bad about it at first, then after a while I didn't think about it anymore.

Another of the biblical greats was Elijah. Who else in biblical or modern times possessed enough courage to issue a challenge by standing alone against 450 prophets?

He confronted King Ahab and the prophets of the god Baal and mocked them when their god failed to answer their prayers. He built a stone altar with his own hands, killed a young bull, cut it in pieces, and laid it on the altar. God honored him by sending fire from heaven, giving him victory in the contest.

After all that, the threat of one woman caused him to run for his life. Admittedly she was a queen with great influence over her husband, and she fully intended to make good her threat. But after the challenges he had faced and overcome, it seems of little consequence.

Yet I think I know why Elijah fled. I've learned that in the middle of an emotional high, maybe even a great spiritual victory, we're charged with adrenaline. Then afterward we find ourselves drained, exhausted, and vulnerable. That's when I—and many others—have fallen prey to temptations and failures.

What about Peter? For all his effrontery, the first time he was really put to the test, he failed. "I don't even know him," he said of Jesus.

If we look at the end of the Gospels, it seems that Jesus' mission failed because of the small group of men who couldn't stand up for him. And yet later—when they were infused with the Holy Spirit—failure performed some kind of miracle in their characters. They ended up carrying the message of Jesus to every part of the earth. And they were committed enough to be willing to be fed to lions, used as human torches, drawn and quartered, beheaded, boiled in oil, or dismembered and sawn in half.

The power to choose is one aspect of humanity being created in the image of God. With the power to choose comes the power to fail.

And we all fail. We can despair or, like the true heroes and heroines of God, we can use our failures as steppingstones to lead us more firmly on God's solid pathway of light.